# MICROSERVICES FOR
# BEGINNERS

## Disclaimer

All erudition supplied in this publication are defined for scholastic and instructional purposes only. The writer is never liable for any outcomes that emerge from utilizing this publication. Constructive initiatives have been made to render details that are both effective and precise; nonetheless, the author is not to be held accountable or responsible for any use/misuse of this information.

# FOREWORD

I sincerely thank you for taking the very first significant step of trusting me and determining to purchase/read this life-transforming publication. Thanks for investing your time and your hard-earned resources on this book.

I can assure you of accurate results if you will vigilantly adhere to the particular plan I lay bare in the well-detailed book you are presently having before you. It has transformed lives, and I highly believe it will similarly change your own life also.

All the detail given in this Do It Yourself piece is easy to assimilate and comprehend.

## TABLE OF CONTENTS

# INTRODUCTION

The scope of the book is significant, as the ramifications of fine-grained microservice architectures are also broad. As such, it needs to attract people interested in aspects of style, advancement, implementation, testing, and maintenance of various systems. Some people have already embarked on the journey towards microservices architectures, whether for a greenfield application or as part of decaying an existing, more monolithic system, will discover a lot of useful advice to help you. It will likewise assist those of you who need to know what all the difficulty has to do with, so that you can figure out whether microservices are ideal for you.

Microservices is a fast-moving topic. Although the concept is not brand-new (even if the term itself is), experiences from individuals all over the world, in addition to the emergence of brand-new technologies, are having a profound result on how they are utilized. Due to the fast lane of modification, I ensure to focus this book on concepts more than particular technologies, knowing that application information constantly changes quicker than other systems. This book is arranged in a topic-based format. As such, you may desire to leap into the specific topics that intrigue you the most.

# CHAPTER ONE

## UNDERSTANDING MICROSERVICES

For numerous years now, we have been finding much better ways to construct systems. We have been gaining from what has come before, adopting innovations, and observing how a new age of technology companies operate in different methods to produce IT systems that help make both their clients and their designers happier.

Microservices has taken the application advancement industry by a storm. It has left a significant influence on the companies by bringing many significant advantages. Application of the microservices is more of an art than a science.

Application developers typically discover it hard to get a catch on what's and how's of a well-designed microservice architecture. You must have heard of microservices in several times. But this time, we are advancing on the extensive details for microservices. This book will act as a helping hand for those who would like to know this container-based architecture in the information.

What are Microservices?

Illustration image revealing a difference in between microservices and monolithic architecture with light pink colored cubes having various services in several colors.

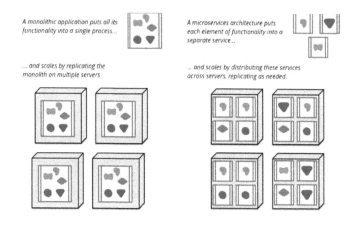

Microservices, is the buzzword of the modern software advancement architecture, has taken place above Agile, DevOps, and RESTful services. Martin Fowler describes Microservices as a technique to develop a single application as the suites of small deployable services.

Each service runs in its own set of processes and communicates through numerous light-weight protocols

(HTTP resource API). The services are developed around an organization, around organisation abilities and are released utilizing a piece of fully automated implementation machinery. In addition, there occurs a decentralized control and management of services that are written in various programs languages and utilize distinct information storage innovations.

Dr. Peter Rogers used the term 'micro web services' throughout a conference on cloud computing (2005). Prior to moving any even more, let's have an appearance at the series of occasions that formed the early software development patterns and resulted in the production of microservices.

## The approach behind Microservices

A monolithic application is a one deployable unit incorporating different elements that are enclosed to form a single workable environment. The database, client-side user interface layer, and server-side applications are the elements of a monolithic application. Everyone understands Java program language which comes as a standalone plan and takes numerous formats EAR, WAR, JAR that are shared as a uniformed unit on the application server.

Object-oriented fundamental assumptions are used for building monolithic applications that streamline the advancement, release, debugging, and testing processes. This works well if the applications remain in their preliminary phases and the structure is more streamlined. As the size of the application increases, class hierarchies, and interdependencies in-between parts increases leading to an intricate application.

The increasing intricacy makes monolithic applications an undesirable choice for the cloud environment, the following points support this fault isolation is challenging: As pointed out previously, being a single deployable system there is no physical separation in between the different functional locations (for example, a single function is reliant on the functionality of another feature) of a monolithic system. Hence, no single release will guarantee that it will just affect the location they targeted. Therefore, unintended side-effects are always a possibility when it comes to a monolithic application.

- Growth needs more resources:

Even for the addition of a small feature or functionality, a monolithic application requires a couple of additional resources. In many of the cases, expansion or scaling of a monolithic application is done by deploying multiple instances of the whole application as soon as.

Implementation consumes a great deal of time: With the increasing intricacy, the advancement and QA cycles for a monolithic application requires more time than typical. Any regular changes at the time of implementation are not recommended for the monolithic applications as it needs an application restore, complete regression screening, and release of the whole monolithic application again. This entire process takes in a great deal of time and likewise is quite complicated to take forward.

- Using the same innovation over and over

The tendency of a monolithic application to describe a single innovation stack poses lots of difficulties. The layers of a monolithic application are firmly combined in-process calls. In order to keep the information exchange structured, the very same innovation stack is utilized, therefore unable to take advantage of the new and existing innovation stack.

For the function of resolving the issues of the monolithic applications, Microservices became a prime upgrade to boost the ROI for the industries moving to the cloud.

Before going more deeply into the book,let's understand the what, how and why, of the microservices, let's take a look at the growing appeal of microservices in the past 5 years from the listed below Google Trends graph.

## The Evolution of Microservices

In order to understand the gradual increase of a microservice architecture, it is essential to go back to the timeline and check out how and where all of it started. The below-written series of occasions has been put together by IBM and we have bifurcated them on the basis of the accompanying observations.

Observation 1: Everything that is distributed does not indicate that it ought to be distributed.

Early 1980 saw the arrival of Remote Procedure Calls (RPC) by Sun Microsystems that were based on ONC RPC (Open Network Computing Remote Procedure Call) and the concepts of DCE (Distributed Computing Environment, 1988) and CORBA (Common Object Request Broker Architecture, 1991). The fundamental of these innovations was to make remote calls transparent for the developers. The large machine-crossing systems were developed to avoid processing and memory expansion problems while invoking remote or regional RPCs.

Gradually, the local space addresses became more significant with the improving processors. A crucial observation entered into the point of view with this big set of DCE and CORBA execution, that is, if something can be distributed it doesn't suggest that it needs to be dispersed. Martin Fowler later on explained this as microservices that ought to be organized around company capabilities.

As the large memory areas became a regular thing system performances were negatively impacted by the inadequate approaches distribution. Earlier the little memory space resulted in numerous chatty user interfaces. However the systems having significant memory spaces circulation advantages, exceeded the networking overheads.

Observation 2: The collapse of a local distributed call.

The pattern was used in distributed systems and on the rough user interfaces of entire subsystems, therefore exposing only those which are offered for circulation. The whole concept of a Facade pattern defines a specific external API for a system or subsystem that needs to be business-driven.

An API is an abbreviation for Applications Programming Interface is a framework that helps with discussions in between 2 applications. APIs allow developers to either gain access to application information or use their performance. Technically speaking, an API sends out data by methods of HTTP requests. The textual action is returned in the JSON format. REST, SOAP, GraphQL, gRPC are the few API style styles. OpenAPI, RAML, or AsyncAPI are the other spec formats that are used to define API interactions in machine-readable and human formats.

A service-oriented architecture can be defined as a multiple-use and synchronously interacting services and APIs. These facilitate the paced application advancement procedure and simple data incorporation from other systems.

SOAP was all about item methods invocation over HTTP and facilitated debugging and logging of text-based networking calls. SOAP promoted heterogeneous interoperability but failed in handling methods other than simple approach invocation like exception handling, transaction assistance, security, and digital signatures.

Observation 3: Self-contained runtime and environments.

Slowly the procedural, layered principles of SOAP and the WS-* requirements location were obtained by Representational State Transfer (REST). REST focused on using the HTTP verbs, as they were specified to develop, read, delete, and update semantics. Along with this, it defined a method to identify unique entity names called the Uniform Resource Identifier (URI), the very same time saw the rejection of another tradition of the Java Platform, Java Enterprise Edition (JEE) and SOA. At the time of its introduction, JEE led numerous corporations to embrace the concept of using an application server as a host for several different applications. A single operations group managed, monitored, and maintained a group of identical application servers, typically from Oracle or IBM to perform the deployment of various department applications onto that group, reducing the expense of the general operation.

The application developers had a hard time to deal with large-sized development and test environments. It is owing to the reality that the settings were hard to develop and needed operations teams for their functioning. Inconsistencies had been seen between application server versions, patch levels, application information, and software application setups between environments. The open-source application servers (Tomcat or Glassfish) were preferred by the designers as they were smaller sized in size and light-weight application platforms.

All at once, the complexity of the JEE operated in favor of the platform as meth0ods like Inversion of Control and Dependency Injection became typical. The development teams discovered that they were on a useful side in having their independent runtime environments which resulted in decentralized governance and information management. The series of occasions hence took place caused a strong foundation for the microservices adoption by the enterprises.

**Microservices Features**

Componentization Improves Scalability

With microservices, the applications are developed by breaking services into different parts. This leads to the smooth alterations, advancement, and implementation of service on its own. The least reliance state of the microservices comes as an advantage for the developers as modifications and redeployments or scaling can be done on the particular parts of the application rather than on the entire code. Therefore, the performance and availability of business-critical services can be improved by releasing them into several servers without impacting the efficiency of other services.

## Sensible Functional Borders and Boosted Strength

As pointed out previously in microservices, the entire application is decentralized and decoupled into services. When and where the modification has happened, this sets the borders in between services and likewise a level of modularity so that designers have a concept. Similarly, unlike monolithic style, any tweak in the capability of service will not impact the other parts of the application, and also even if several parts of the system failure, will go unnoticed by the individuals.

## Fail-Safe with Easier Debugging and Testing

Applications created using microservices are smart enough to deal with failures. The failed service happily gets out of the method if a single service stops working amongst numerous interacting services.

Failure can be discovered with the constant monitoring of the microservices. With the continuous delivery and screening process, the circulation of error-free applications scales up.

## Increased ROI and Reduced TCO with Resource Optimization

In microservices, numerous teams work on independent services facilitating the quick deployment of the application. A constant delivery design is followed enabling developers, operations, and testing groups to work at the same time on a single service.

Costly machines or systems are not required for the operation of these decoupled services, first x86 devices do the work. This resource optimization and continuous delivery and deployment improve the performance of microservices lowering the infrastructure expenses and downtime, eventually leading to the shipment of the application into the marketplace at a fast speed.

**Flexible Tool Selection**

Dependences on a single vendor are not the case for microservices. Instead, there is a versatility to utilize a tool according to the tasks. Each service is complimentary to use its language framework, or auxiliary services while still being in communication with the other services in the application.

**Communication in Microservices**

The basic concept of inter-service interaction is, two mioroservices interacting with each other either through HTTP procedure or asynchronous message patterns.

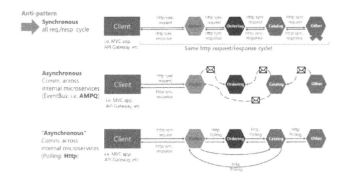

The primary two types of inter-service communication in microservices are explained:

Illustration image above showing a flowchart to develop order circulation with asynchronous and simultaneous interaction having numerous parts in various colors

## Concurrent Communication

Two services interact with each other through a rest endpoint utilizing an HTTP or HTTPs protocol. In synchronous communication, the calling service waits until the caller service reacts.

## Asynchronous Communication

The communication is performed asynchronous messaging. In asynchronous messaging, the calling service will not have to wait on the action from the caller service. Initially, a response to a user is returned and after that the remaining requests are processed. Apache Kafka, Apache ActiveMQ is used for carrying out asynchronous communication in microservices.

## Factors To Consider for Microservices Architecture Building

At the exceptionally first, a blueprint or structure is required for the effective building of a microservices architecture. In order to produce a structure based on domains, it can be divided into the following elements or verticals:

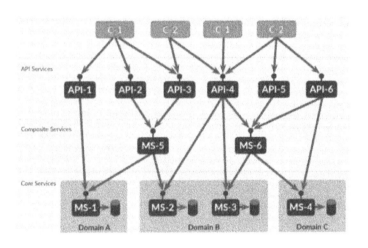

**Central Services:** It applies the rules for business and the other logic. Service information consistency is dealt with by a central service.

Composite Services: For the function of carrying out a comparable or common task and any information accumulation from different primary services, composite services carry the company treatment of the primary services.

API Providers: Allowing 3rd celebrations to develop creative applications that will make use of the first performance in the system landscape.

In addition to the structure, a target architecture requires to be defined before scaling the microservices. The factor is to avoid the disturbance of the IT landscape leading to its underperformance.

## Things to Consider while Switching to Microservices

The shift from monoliths to microservices does not happen fortnight. Adrian Cockcroft, a microservices evangelist and known for the introduction of microservices at Netflix, has noted the following best practices for designing and implementation of microservices architecture inside a company.

Concentrate On Enhancing Organisation Competency:

While dealing with microservices, it is recommended for the groups to know diverse requirements for specific company abilities. For instance, approval of the order, delivering so regarding handle the delivery of an item. Additionally, services must be developed as independent products with significant paperwork, each one accountable for a single business capability.

Comparable Maturity Level for all Codes:

All the code that is composed in microservice needs to have the same level of maturity and stability. If there is a scenario of the addition or rewording of code for a microservice, the most beneficial method is to leave the existing microservice and create a brand-new microservice for the brand-new or transformed system. This does the release and testing of a new code until it is error-free and efficient.

No Single Data Store:

The information shop ought to be picked as per the requirements from each microservices group. A single database source for each microservice will bring few excessive dangers, for instance, an update on the database will get reflected in every service accessing that database regardless of its relevance or not.

Container Implementation:

The implementation in containers leads to the use of a single tool that helps with the delivery of a microservice. Docker is one of the most chosen container these days.

Stateless Servers:  Servers can be replaced based on the requirement or in any ill-functionality.

Display Everything: Microservices is made up of a lot of moving areas and therefore, it is vital to perform appropriate tracking of whatever under consideration such as response time alerts, service error notices, and dashboards. Splunk and AppDynamics come as a help in the microservices measuring procedure.

There is no doubt that microservices are a hot pattern for the present application development generation, however it does bring a few drawbacks associated with it.

**The Microservices Drawbacks**

Below are noted some possible downsides associated with microservices.

Due to the independent services, each demand requires to be managed carefully and likewise the communication between modules requires extra care. The implementation of microservices can be troublesome and requires total coordination amongst different microservices.

1. Cumbersome Data Management:

With the presence of numerous databases, it ends up being quite uncontrollable to deal with transactions and management of a database shop.

2. Inconvenient Testing:

The dependence between services requires to be verified before performing the testing of microservices, that is, robust tracking and testing are crucial.

Tools to Handle Microservices

The look for the right tools is vital prior to construct a microservices application. A broad range of open-source and paid tools are offered that assistance microservices building. It has always been stated that microservices advancement shines brilliantly with the provided open-source tools. Below are listed the few tools for developing a microservices application:

Red Hat OpenShift-- The Red Hat Openshift is an easily dispersed multiple container application platform from Red Hat Inc. An application reinforcing Kubernetes application with Docker containers is being used commonly for advancement, deployment, and management of applications on hybrid, cloud and within the enterprises.

Mesosphere: Mesosphere is a dispersed computer running system for handling clusters. The container platform is built around the open-source kernel Apache Mesos and Mesosphere's DC/OS (Information Center Operating System). The robust, versatile and platform containerization platform performs intensive tasks within a business. The diagram below programs the components of the Mesosphere.

Instana-- The dynamic application performance management system which carries out the automatic monitoring of constantly altering contemporary applications. It has been created mainly for the cloud-native stack and carries out infrastructure and application performance monitoring with no configuration effort and hence accelerating the CI/CD (continuous integration/continuous deployment) cycle. The diagram below shows an Instana dependency map for demo store containers.

Have a look at the more open-source tools to manage microservices applications

The Future:

Microservices are Entering Mainstream

Netflix, eBay, Twitter, PayPal, and Amazon are the few big names that have acquired a strong market presence by shifting from a monolithic architecture to a microservices.

A survey (2015) with the concern, 'Which declaration 'best' defines how your company is presently utilizing microservices?' by Nginx states that near about 70% of the organizations are either utilizing or are doing a research study on microservices, with almost one third are currently using them in the production.

Service fits together, event-driven architectures, container-native security, GraphQL, and mayhem engineering were the microservices patterns for the year 2018. The quick increase of microservices has brought a few new trends into the vision. Below are discussed the 2019 predictions for microservices:

1. Test Automation

Checking is performed to inspect the health of an application. Services always aspire for the screening services that create runs, and report the results automatically. Together with this, testing must be smooth and need to help with connections to CI systems, brand-new code check-in real-time, and addition of comments similar to a human engineer.

The expert systems will take advantage of many take advantage of software screening, specifically, enhances efficiency, expense, accuracy, and coverage.

2. Continuous Deployment and Enhanced Productivity with Verification.

With Continuous Deployment the code is immediately deployed to the production environment after it successfully passes the screening phase. A set of design practices are used in Continuous Deployment to press the code into the production environment.

Furthermore, with Continuous Verification (CV) occasion data from logs and APMs are collected. In order to understand the functions that caused success and failed implementations.

3.  Addressing Failures with Incident reactions.

The complex dispersed architectures are frequently delicate. The website reliability engineers (SRE) are accountable for the schedule, latency, efficiency, effectiveness, change management, tracking, emergency response, and capability preparation of the services. The incident action is an essential SRE job. When a service stops working, a team with distinct roles addresses and handles the after-effects of the failures.

4.  Save Dollars with Cloud Service Expense Management (CSEM).

Cloud cost administration is among the few difficulties that affect both the engineering, IT groups, and the whole business. Cloud Service Expense Management screens and manages the cloud-computing expenditures and the cloud resources that will help business to obtain the very best value for their services.

5. Expansion of Machine Learning with Kubernetes.

Kubernetes is slowly growing and is entering into the artificial intelligence (ML) stack. Numerous companies are working on to standardize on Kubernetes or ML and analytical work.

A scientist Eric Evans's assisted in comprehending the significance of representing the real-life in our code, and showed us better ways to design our systems. The concept of microservices revealed how we could more effectively and productively get software into production, instilling in the idea that we should deal with every check-in as a release prospect.

Virtualization platforms enabled us to provision and resize our devices at will, with infrastructure automation giving us a way to deal with these machines at scale. Some big, successful organizations like Amazon and Google espoused the view of small groups owning the complete lifecycle of their services. And, more recently, Netflix has shared with us ways of building antifragile systems at a scale that would have been tough to comprehend merely ten years earlier. Many organizations have discovered that by welcoming fine-grained, microservice architectures, they can deliver software applications faster and embrace more recent technologies.

Microservices provide us substantially more flexibility to react and make different decisions, enabling us to respond faster to the unavoidable change that impacts everyone.

Microservices are small, autonomous services that work together. Let's break that meaning down a bit and consider the attributes that make microservices different. They are little, and focused on doing one thing well.

Codebases grow as we write code to add brand-new functions. In time, it can be tough to because the codebase is so big, know where a modification requires to be made

When it concerns how little is little enough, I like to believe in these terms: the smaller the service, the more you optimize the advantages and downsides of microservice architecture.

**Autonomous.**

The microservice is a different entity, it might be released as an isolated service on a platform as a service (PAAS), or it might be its os process. Scientists try to avoid loading multiple services onto the same device, although the definition of invention in today's world is pretty hazy! As we'll go over later, although this seclusion can include some overhead, the resulting simplicity makes our dispersed system a lot easier to reason about, and newer innovations can mitigate numerous of the obstacles associated with this type of implementation.

All communication between the services themselves is via network calls, to impose separation in between the services and prevent the dangers of tight coupling.

These services require to be able to change separately and be released by themselves without requiring customers to switch. We need to consider what our services must expose, and what they must allow being hidden. If there is excessive sharing, our consuming services become coupled to our internal representations, this decreases our autonomy, as it requires extra coordination with consumers when

making modifications.

The service exposes an application programming interface (API), and collaborate services using those APIs. We'll return time and again to the value of useful, decoupled APIs throughout this book.

**Secret Benefits.**

The benefits of microservices are many and different. A number of these advantages can be laid at the door of any dispersed system. Microservices, nevertheless, tend to attain these benefits to a higher degree primarily due to how far they take the principles behind distributed systems and service-oriented architecture.

1. Technology Heterogeneity.

With a system made up of numerous, teaming up services, we can decide to use different technologies inside everyone. This enables us to choose the right tool for each job, instead of having to select a more standardized, one-size-fits-all approach that often winds up being the most affordable standard measure.

We may choose to use various innovation that is much better achieve to attain performance efficiency required if one part of our system needs to improve its efficiency.

We may also decide that how we store our data requires to alter for various parts of our system. For a social network, we might save our users' interactions in a graph-oriented database to reflect the highly interconnected nature of a social graph possibly the posts the users make could be stored in a document-oriented data shop, giving rise to a heterogeneous architecture like the one displayed in Figure below

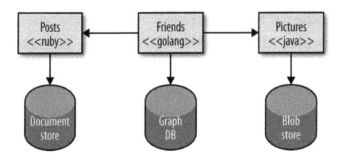

With microservices, we are likewise able to embrace technology faster, and comprehend how new advancements may help us. Among the most significant barriers to attempting out and adopting innovation is the threats connected with it. With a monolithic application, if you want to try a new program database, language, or structure, any modification will impact a significant amount of my system. With a system including several services,

Many organizations find this ability to absorb neTechnologieses to be a real advantage for them quickly. Embracing multiple innovations does not come without an overhead, of course. Some companies pick to put some constraints on language choices. Netflix and Twitter, primarily use the Java Virtual Machine (JVM) as a platform, as they have very really excellent of the reliability and performance of that system. They establish libraries and tooling for the JVM that make running at scale much easier, however make it more hard for non-Java-based services or clients. Neither

Twitter nor Netflix usage only one innovation stack for all tasks, either. Another counterpoint to issues about mixing in various technologies is the size. , if I truly can reword my microservice in 2 weeks, you may well mitigate the dangers of welcoming new innovation.

As you'll discover throughout this book, simply like numerous things worrying microservices, it's everything about discovering the ideal balance. We'll discuss how to make innovation choices in, you'll learn how to guarantee that your services can evolve their technology independently of each other without excessive coupling.

2. Durability.

A key idea in resilience engineering is the bulkhead. If one element of a system fails, but that failure does not cascade, you can isolate the problem and the rest of the service boundaries become your apparent bulkheads. However with microservices, we can develop systems that handle the overall failure of services and break down performance accordingly.

One needs to be cautious, to ensure the microservice systems can properly embrace this enhanced strength, we need to understand the brand-new sources of failure that dispersed systems need to deal with. Networks can and will stop working, as will devices. You need to understand how to manage this, and what impact (if any) it must have on completion user of our software application.

3. Scaling.

With a big, microservice, we have to scale whatever together. One little part of our total system is constrained in performance, but if that habits is locked up in a large application, we have to handle scaling whatever as a piece. With smaller services, we can simply scale those services that need scaling, permitting us to run other parts of the system on smaller sized, less powerful hardware, like in Figure

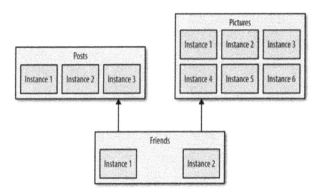

Example: Gilt, an online style retailer, embraced microservices for this precise reason. Beginning in 2007 with a Rails application, by 2009 Gilt's system

was not able to deal with the load being placed on it. By splitting out core parts of its system, Gilt was better able to offer with its traffic spikes, and today has over 450 microservices, each one running on numerous separate makers.

When welcoming on-demand provisioning systems like those provided by Amazon Web Services, we can even apply this scaling as needed for those pieces that need it, this allows us to manage our expenses more effectively.

4. Relief of Deployment.

A one-line modification to a million-line-long monolithic application requires the whole application to be deployed to release the modification. That might be a large-impact, high-risk deployment. In practice, large-impact, leads to high-risk, which end up occasionally happening due to reasonable worry. With microservices, we can modify a single service and deploy it independently of the remainder of the system. This permits us to get our code released faster, if an issue does take place, it can be isolated quickly to an individual service, making quick rollback easy to accomplish. It likewise indicates we can get our new performance out to consumers much faster. This is one of the primary reasons organizations like Amazon and Netflix use these architectures-- to ensure they eliminate as numerous obstacles as possible to getting software out the door.

The innovation in this area has altered significantly in the last number of years, and we'll be looking more deeply into the subject of implementation in a microservice world.

5. Organizational Alignment.

Many of us have experienced the problems connected with big teams and big codebases. These problems can be intensified when the unit is distributed. We also know that smaller sized organizations dealing with smaller sized codebases tend to be more productive.

Microservices permit us to align our architecture to our company better, helping us decrease the variety of people dealing with anyone codebase to strike the sweet area of the team size and efficiency. The ownership of services between groups can be moved to keep individuals working on one facility colocated.

6. Composability.

One of the key guarantees of dispersed systems and service-oriented architectures is that it opens up chances for reuse of functionality. With microservices, it enables your performance to be consumed in various methods for various purposes. This can be especially essential when we believe about how our consumers utilize our software. Gone is the time when we could think narrowly about either our desktop website or mobile application.

### 7. Optimizing for Replaceability

Teams using microservice techniques are comfortable with completely rewriting services when needed, and just eliminating a service when it is no longer required. When a codebase is simply a few hundred lines long, it is difficult for individuals to become mentally connected to it, and the cost of replacing it is pretty small.

### Service-Oriented Architecture

Service-oriented architecture (SOA) is a design method where several services work together to provide some end set of capabilities. A service here generally suggests an entirely different operating system process. Communication between these services happens via calls across a network rather than approach calls within a procedure boundary.

SOA became an approach to combat the obstacles of the large monolithic applications. It is a technique that aims to promote the reusability of software; 2 or more end-user applications, for instance, both utilize the exact same services. It aims to make it much easier to preserve or reword software, as theoretically we can replace one service Without anybody knowing, as long as the semantics of the service does not change excessive. SOA is an extremely sensible idea. However, regardless of numerous efforts, there is a lack of excellent agreement on how to do SOA well. In my viewpoint, much of the industry has actually failed to look holistically enough at the issue and provide a compelling option to the narrative set out by various suppliers in this area.

Much of the issues laid at the door of SOA are actually issues with things like communication protocols (e.g., SOAP), supplier middleware, a lack of assistance about service granularity, or the wrong help on choosing places to split your system. The microservice method has actually emerged from real-world usage, taking our better understanding of systems and architecture to do SOA well. You must think of microservices as a specific approach for SOA in the same method that XP or Scrum are particular approaches for Agile software application development.

The Open Source Gateway Initiative (OSGI) is worth calling out as one technologyspecific technique to modular decomposition. Java itself doesn't have a real concept of modules, and we'll have to wait at least till Java 9 to see this contributed to the language. OSGI, which emerged as a structure to enable plug-ins to be set up in the Eclipse Java. IDE, is now used as a method to retrofit a module concept in Java via a library.

The issue with OSGI is that it is attempting to impose things like module lifecycle management without enough assistance in the language itself. This results in more work needing to be done by module authors to provide on correct module seclusion. Within a process border, it is also a lot easier to fall under the trap of making modules excessively coupled to each other, causing all sorts of problems.

Hopefully by now you understand what a microservice is, what makes it various from other compositional strategies, and what a few of the essential advantages are. In each of the following chapters we will enter into more detail on how to attain these advantages and how to avoid some of the typical risks. There are a variety of subjects to cover, however we require to begin someplace. Among the primary obstacles that microservices introduce is a shift in the role of those who frequently directs the development of our systems.

# CHAPTER TWO

## ARCHITECT MINDSET ON MICROSERVICES

As we have seen so far, microservices offer us a lot of choices, and accordingly a lot of options to make. With the faster speed of change in the environment it enables architectures, the role of the designer to change. In this chapter, I'll take a relatively opinionated view of the role of a designer.

Architects have a crucial task, they are in charge of ensuring we have a joined-up technical vision, it is a need to help us provide the system our consumers require. In others, they may be defining the vision for a whole program of work, coordinating with multiple groups throughout the world, or maybe even an entire company. At whatever level they run, the function is challenging one to pin down, and regardless of it being the apparent professional development for designers in companies, it is also a function that gets more criticism than practically any other.

More than any other function, designers can have a direct effect on the quality of the systems constructed, on the working conditions of their coworkers, and on their organization's ability to react to change, and yet we so often seem to get this function incorrect. Why is that?

The microservices market is a child, this is something we seem to forget, and yet we have just been producing programs that work on what we acknowledge as computer systems for around 70 years.

We are continuously looking to other occupations in an attempt to explain what we do. We aren't medical physicians or engineers, but nor are we plumbers or electrical experts. Instead, we fall into some happy medium, which makes it difficult for society to understand us, or for us to know where we fit. So we borrow from other professions. We call ourselves software application "engineers," or " architects."

Strategic Goals.

The role of the designer is already intimidating enough, so luckily we typically do not need to define tactical goals! Strategic objectives ought to talk to where your business is going, and how it sees itself making its customers happy. These will be essential objectives, and may not consist of innovation at all. They could be defined at a company level or a division level. They might be things like "Expand into Southeast Asia to open brand-new markets," or "Let the client accomplish as much as possible using self-service." The key is that this is where your organization is headed, so you require to ensure the technology is aligned to it. If you're the person specifying the company's technical vision, this might suggest you'll need to spend more time with the nontechnical parts of your organization. What is the driving vision for the organization? And how does it alter? These questions must be properly answered.

Principles

Principles are regulations you have made in order to align what you are doing to some larger objective, as well as will certainly sometimes transform. As an example, if among your strategic objectives as an organization is to reduce the time to market for brand-new attributes, you might define a concept

that states that distribution teams have complete control over the lifecycle of their software program to ship whenever they are ready, separately of any other group. If one more goal is that your company is relocating to boldy grow its offering in various other countries, you might choose to apply a concept that the whole system should be portable to permit it to be released locally in order to respect sovereignty of data.

HTTP/REST is a common integration style. As a result of their technological nature, practices will frequently transform regularly than principles.

Similar to principles, occasionally methods show constraints in your organization. For example, if you sustain only CentOS, this will undoubtedly require to be shown in your techniques.

Part of what architects need to handle is administration. What do I indicate by governance? It

ends up the Control Purposes for Information and also Related Modern Technology (COBIT) has a correct interpretation:.

Governance guarantees that business purposes are attained by evaluating stakeholder requirements, problems and options; setting direction with prioritisation and choice making; and monitoring efficiency, compliance and development against agreed-on.

instructions and also objectives.

COBIT 5.

Governance can relate to numerous things in the forum of IT. We intend to focus on the.

facet of technological administration, something I feel is the work of the architect. If among the.

engineer's tasks is making sure there is a technical vision, after that administration is about making sure.

what we are building suits this vision, and advancing the vision if required.

Architects are in charge of a great deal of things. They need to guarantee there is a collection of.

concepts that can direct development, which these principles match the organization's.

method. They need to see to it too that these concepts do not call for working.

methods that make designers miserable. They require to maintain to date with new.

modern technology, and know when to make the right trade-offs. This is a horrible great deal of.

obligation. All that, as well as they also require to lug people with them-- that is, to make certain.

that the associates they are dealing with comprehend the choices being made and are.

brought in to carry them out. Oh, and also as we've already stated: they need to spend.

a long time with the groups to understand the effect of their decisions, and also perhaps also.

code too.

A tall order? Absolutely. But I am strongly of the viewpoint that they shouldn't do this alone.

An effectively functioning governance group can collaborate to share the job as well as shape.

the vision.

Normally, administration is a team activity. Maybe an informal conversation with a tiny sufficient.

team, or a much more organized normal meeting with formal group subscription for a bigger.

range. This is where I assume the concepts we covered earlier need to be reviewed as well as.

changed as called for. This team requires to be led by an engineer, as well as to be composed.

predominantly of people who are executing the work being regulated. This team should.

likewise be in charge of tracking as well as handling technical threats.

A design I substantially favor is having the designer chair the group, however having the mass of the.

group drawn from the engineers of each distribution team-- the leads of each group at a.

minimum. The designer is in charge of ensuring the team works, however the group as a.

whole is accountable for administration. This shares the lots, and also makes sure that there is a.

higher degree of buy-in. It also makes sure that information moves freely from the groups into the.

team, and also therefore, the decision making is a lot more practical and notified.

Often, the group may choose with which the engineer differs. At this.

point, what is the architect to do? Having actually remained in this setting before, I can tell you this is.

among one of the most challenging circumstances to face. Frequently, I take the approach that I need to go.

with the group choice. I take the sight that I have actually done my ideal to encourage people, yet.

eventually I had not been encouraging sufficient. The team is frequently much wiser than the individual,.

and I have actually been proven wrong more than as soon as! And imagine exactly how disempowering it can be.

for a team to have actually been offered space to come up with a decision, and after that ultimately be.

ignored. Yet occasionally I have overthrown the team. Yet why, and when? Just how do you pick.

the lines?

Think about teaching children to ride a bike. You can't ride it for them. You see them wobble, but if you actioned in each time it resembled they might diminish, after that they would certainly never discover, and in any case they fall off far less than you believe they will! Yet if you see them about to drift right into web traffic, or into a close-by pond, after that you need to step in.

Likewise, as an architect, you require to have a firm understanding of when, figuratively, your group is guiding into a pond. You also require to be mindful that even if you understand you are right and also overrule the team, this can undermine your position and likewise make the group really feel that they don't have a say. In some cases the best point is to support a decision you do not agree with. Recognizing when to do this and also when not to is challenging, however is occasionally vital.

Constructing a Team.

Being the bottom line individual responsible for the technical vision of your system and guaranteeing that you're performing on this vision isn't nearly making technology decisions.

It's the people you deal with who will be doing the work. Much of the function of the technical leader has to do with assisting expand them-- to help them understand the vision themselves-- as well as also ensuring that they can be active participants in shaping as well as applying the vision too.

Helping the people around you by themselves job growth can take numerous forms, the majority of which are outside the range of this publication. There is one element, though, where a microservice architecture is particularly pertinent. With larger, monolithic systems, there are fewer possibilities for individuals to step up as well as own something. With microservices, on the other hand, we have several independent codebases that will have their very own independent lifecycles. Aiding people step up by having them take possession of private services prior to approving more duty can be a great means to help them attain their very own occupation objectives, and at the same time lightens the load on whoever supervises!

I am a strong believer that terrific software application originates from terrific people. If you fret just about the innovation side of the equation, you're missing out on way majority of the image.

Summary.

To summarize this phase, below are what I see as the core duties of the transformative engineer:.

Vision.

Make sure there is a clearly interacted technological vision for the system that will aid your system satisfy the requirements of your customers as well as company

Compassion.

Understand the effect of your decisions on your customers and also associates.

Cooperation.

Involve with as a lot of your peers as well as associates as possible to assist specify, improve,.as well as perform the vision.

Adaptability.

Ensure that the technological vision modifications as your clients or company needs it.

Autonomy.

Locate the right equilibrium between standardizing and allowing autonomy for your teams.

Administration.

Guarantee that the system being carried out fits the technical vision.

The transformative designer is one who recognizes that managing this feat is a constant balancing act. Pressures are always pressing you somehow, as well as understanding where to push back or where to go with the flow is typically something that comes only with experience. But the worst reaction to all these forces that push us towards adjustment is to become extra stiff or dealt with in our thinking.

While much of the recommendations in this chapter can put on any kind of systems engineer, microservices provide us much more decisions to make. Therefore, being better able to balance all of these trade-offs is essential.

In the following chapter, we'll take some of our newly found awareness of the engineer's function with us as we begin thinking of how to find the ideal borders for our microservices.

# CHAPTER THREE

## DESIGNING SCALABLE BACKEND INFRASTRUCTURES FROM SCRATCH

When establishing the first version of an application, you typically do not have any scalability concerns. Using a distributed architecture slows down advancement.

Distribute API advancement: The system should be designed in a method such that numerous groups can deal with it at the same time and a single group need to not become a bottleneck nor does it needs to have competence on the entire application to produce optimised endpoints.

Support multiple languages: In order to take advantage of emerging technologies every functional part of the system must have the ability to support the favored language of option for that performance.

Decrease latency: Any architecture that we propose must constantly attempt to minimize customer's reaction time.

Reduce release threats: Different functional elements of the system must have the ability to deploy independently with minimal coordination.

Minimize hardware footprint: System ought to try to enhance the quantity of hardware utilized and ought to be horizontally scalable.

Building Monolithic Applications

Let's imagine that you were beginning to develop a brand brand-new eCommerce application planned to take on Amazon. You would begin by producing a new job in your favored choice of platform such as Rails, Spring Boot, Play etc. It would typically have a modular architecture something like this:

Fig 1

The top layer will usually deal with the customer demands and after doing some validations it will forward the demand to service layer where all the business reasoning is carried out. A service will make usage of different adapters like database access components in DAO layer, messaging components, external APIs or other services in the very same layer to prepare the outcome and return it back to the controller which intern returns it to the client.

This sort of application is generally packaged and released as a monolith, indicating one big file. For e.g. it'll be a jar in case of spring boot and a zip file in case of Rails or Node.js app. Applications like these are quite typical and have numerous benefits, they are simple to understand, manage, develop, test and deploy. You can also scale them by running numerous copies of it behind a load balancer and it works rather well up to a particular level.

This simple method has substantial limitations like:

Language/Framework lock: Since entire application is composed in single tech stack. Can' t explore emerging innovations.

Tough to Digest: Once the app becomes large it becomes tough for a designer to understand such a large codebase.

Difficult to distribute API advancement: It becomes very challenging to do agile development and a big part of the developer's time is lost in solving conflicts.

Release as a single unit: Can not individually deploy a single modification to a single component. Modifications are "imprisoned" by other modifications.

Development slows down: I've dealt with a codebase which had more than 50,000 classes. The sheer size of the codebase sufficed to decrease the IDE and startup times due to which efficiency utilized to suffer.

Resources are not optimized: Some module might execute CPU-intensive image processing reasoning needing compute-optimized instances and another module might be an in-memory database and finest fit for Memory-optimized circumstances. We'll have to jeopardize on our choice of hardware. Due to the fact that we can't scale a module individually, it may also happen that one module of application requires scaling but we'll have to run a whole circumstances of the application again.

Wouldn't it be awesome if we could break down the application into smaller parts and manage them in such a method that it acts as a single application when we run it? Yes, it would be and that's exactly what we'll do next!

Microservices Architecture

Numerous companies, such as Amazon, Facebook, Twitter, eBay and Netflix have fixed this issue by embracing what is now known as the Microservices Architecture pattern It tackles this issue by dividing it into smaller sub-problems aka divide and conquer in designers world. Look at figure 1 carefully, we'll cut vertical slices out of it and produce smaller interconnected services. Each slice will implement a distinct performance such as cart management, user management and order management etc. Each service can be composed in any language/framework and can have the polyglot determination that suits the usage case. Easy-peasy?

However wait! We likewise wanted it to act like a single application to the client otherwise, client will have to handle all the complexity that includes this architecture like aggregating the information from numerous services, preserving so lots of endpoints, increased chattiness of client and server, separate authentication to each service. Client dependence on microservices straight makes it tough to refactor the services also. An intuitive way to do this is to conceal these services behind a new service layer and provide APIs that is customized to each client. This aggregator service layer is also referred to as API Gateway and is a typical method to tackle this issue.

API Gateway based microservices architecture pattern.

All demands from customers first go through the API Gateway. Because this entrance supplies customer specific APIs it lowers the number of round-trips between the client and application which reduces network latency and it also simplifies the client code.

The practical decomposition of the monolith will differ according to the usage case. Amazon utilizes more than 100 microservices to show a single item page whereas Netflix has more than 600 microservices handling their backend. The microservices noted in the above diagram offers you a concept of how a scalable eCommerce application ought to be decomposed but a more careful observation may be needed prior to implementing it for production.

There ain't no such thing as a complimentary lunch. Microservices brings some complex challenges with it, like:

Dispersed Computing Challenges: Since various microservices will need to run in a distributed environment we'll require to look after these Fallacies of Distributed Computing. Simply put, we have to presume that the habits and the areas of the parts of our system will continuously change.

Remote calls are pricey: Developers need to choose and execute an effective inter-process communication mechanism.

Dispersed Transactions: Business deals that upgrade several business entities require to depend on ultimate consistency over ACID.

Handling Service Unavailability: We'll require to design our system to handle unavailability or sluggishness of services. Whatever stops working all the time.

Implementing functions that cover several services.

Integration testing and change management end up being tough.

Naturally, managing complexities of microservices manually will soon start getting out of hands. In order to build a automatic and self-healing distributed system we'll require to have following features in our architecture.

Central Configuration: A centralized, versioned configuration system, something like Zookeeper, alters to which are dynamically applied to running services.

Service discovery: Every running service ought to register itself with a service discovery server and the server tells everybody who is online. Similar to a typical chat app. We don't want to hard-code service endpoint address into one another.

Load balancing: Client side load balancing, so that you can use intricate balancing methods and do caching, batching, fault tolerance, service discovery and handle numerous protocols.

Inter-process communication: We'll require to carry out an efficient inter-process communication method. It can be anything like REST or Thrift or asynchronous, message-based interaction systems such as AMQP or STOMP. We can likewise use efficient message formats such as Avro or Protocol Buffers because this will not be utilized to communicate with outdoors world.

Authentication and security: We need to have a system for identifying authentication requirements for each resource and rejecting requests that do not please them.

Non-blocking IO: API Gateway deals with demands by invoking numerous backend services and aggregating the outcomes. With some requests, such as a product information request, the demands to backend services are independent of one another. In order to lessen response time, the API Gateway ought to perform independent demands simultaneously.

Eventual Consistency: We require to have a system in place to manage organisation deals that span multiple services. When a service updates its database, it ought to publish an event and there should be a Message Broker that guarantees that events are delivered at least once to the subscribing services.

Fault Tolerance: We must avoid the situation where a single fault waterfalls into a system failure. API Gateway ought to never block forever awaiting a downstream service. It ought to deal with failures gracefully and return partial reactions whenever possible.

That's one of the crucial principles of a RESTful service. Given that client just communicates with API Gateway we'll need to run numerous copies of it behind a load balancer since we don't desire API Gateway to become a bottleneck. We do not desire the client to re-authenticate every time its request falls on a various circumstances of API Gateway.

Dispersed caching: We should have caching systems at multiple levels to decrease customer latency. Several levels just implies client, API Gateway and microservices ought to each have a trustworthy caching mechanism.

In-depth tracking: We need to have the ability to track meaningful information and data of each practical part in order to give us an accurate view of production. Appropriate alarms need to be triggered in case of exceptions or high action times.

Dynamic Routing: API Gateway should be able to intelligently route the requests to microservices if it does not have a specific mapping to the asked for resource. To put it simply, modifications should not be required in API Gateway each time a microservice includes a brand-new endpoint on its side.

Vehicle Scaling: Each component of our architecture consisting of API Gateway need to be horizontally scalable and should scale instantly when required even if it is deployed inside a container.

Polyglot Support: Since various microservices may be written in various languages or structures, the system must offer smooth service invocations and above mentioned features regardless of the language it is written in.

Smooth Deployment: Deployment of our microservices need to be quick, independent and automated if possible.

Platform independent: To make effective usage of hardware and to keep our services independent of the platform on which it is released we ought to deploy our web services inside some container like the docker.

Log Aggregation: We ought to have a system in location which immediately keeps aggregating logs from all the microservices onto a file system. These logs might be used for various analytics in the future.

These are lot of functions to implement just to take care of an architecture. The microservices architecture is fight tested by companies like Netflix which alone consumes around 40% of world's web's bandwidth.

# CHAPTER FOUR

## INTEGRATION OF MICROSERVICES

Getting the combination right is the only essential element of the innovation connected with microservices in my viewpoint. Do it well, in other for your microservices to retain their freedom, allowing you to alter as well as launch them independent of the whole. Get it wrong, and face the challenges that are at stake. When you've study this chapter you'll discover exactly how to, with any luck avoid several of the most significant mistakes that have actually tormented various other attempts at SOA and might yet await you in your trip to microservices.

### Looking for the Ideal Integration Technology

There is a bewildering array of alternatives out there for exactly how one microservice can operate to another. Yet which is the ideal one: SOAP? XML-RPC? REST? Protocol buffers? We'll dive into those in a moment, however before we do, let's think about what we want out of whatever technology we select.

Prevent Breaking Changes.

Most times, we may make a change that requires our customers likewise to alter their services. We'll go over just how to handle this later, but we desire to pick technology that ensures this occurs as hardly ever as possible. For instance, if a microservice adds new fields to an item of information it sends out, existing customers shouldn't be affected.

**Keep Your APIs Technology-Agnostic.**

New device structures, as well as languages are appearing all the time, applying originalities that can help us work faster as well as better. Right currently, it could be a.NET shop. What about in a year from now, or five years from now? What happens if you wish to try out a different technology pile that might make you extra efficient?

I am a big fan of keeping my options open, which is why I am such a fan of microservices. It is additionally why I think it is extremely important to ensure that you maintain the APIs made use of for interaction between microservices technology-agnostic. This means preventing the assimilation of modern technology that dictates what technology stacks we can make use of to execute our microservices.

## Make Your Service Simple for Consumers.

We wish to make it very easy for customers to use our service, having it well designed. If the price to utilizing it as a consumer is skies high, microservice doesn't count for much! let's consider what makes it simple for consumers to utilize the remarkable brand-new service.

Preferably, we 'd like to allow our customers full flexibility in their innovation selection, yet on the other hand, providing a customer collection can ease adoption. Typically, however, such collections are inappropriate with other points we wish to attain. For example, we could use client libraries to make it easy for customers, but this can come at the price of enhanced combining.

## Conceal Internal Implementation Detail.

We do not desire our customers to be bound to our internal application. This results in the increased coupling, this implies that if we desire to change something inside our microservice, we can split our customers by needing them to likewise alter. That boosts the expense of modification of the exact outcome we are trying to prevent. It means we are less most likely to wish to make a modification for fear of having to upgrade our customers, which can result in increased technological financial debt within the solution. So any kind of technology that pushes us to subject inner depiction information ought to be prevented.

## Interfacing with Customers.

Since we've got a couple of standards that can assist us pick an excellent technology to utilize for a combination of services, let's look at a few of one of the most usual alternatives out there and attempt to exercise which functions best for us. To help us think this with, let's pick a real-world example from MusicCorp.

Customer production at very first look might be thought about a basic collection of CRUD operations, for many systems it is extra complex than that. Registering a new consumer might require to begin additional processes, like setting up monetary payments or sending welcome emails. As well as when we alter or remove a client, other service processes might get activated too.

So with that said in mind, we must consider some various means in which we may want to work with clients in our MusicCorp system.

**The Shared Database.**

Without a doubt the most usual type of combination that I or any of my associates see in the industry is database (DB) assimilation. In this world, if other services want information from a solution, they reach into the database. As well as if they wish to transform it, they reach into the database! This is truly simple when you initially consider it, and is possibly the fastest form of combination to begin with-- which most likely describes its appeal.

The figure reveals the enrollment UI, which creates consumers by performing SQL operations directly on the database. It likewise shows our telephone call center application that watches and also edits customer information by running SQL on the database. As well as the storehouse updates information about customer orders by querying the database. This is a typical sufficient pattern, but it's one fraught with difficulties.

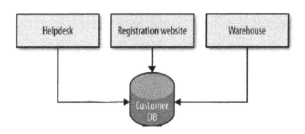

Initially, we are permitting external parties to view and also bind to internal application details. The data structures I keep in the DB are level playing field to all; they are cooperated their entirety with all various other celebrations with access to the data source. If I choose to transform my schema to represent my information far better, or make my system less complicated to keep, I can break my consumers. The DB is properly a very large, common API that is additionally fairly brittle. If I wish to alter the. reasoning associated with, state, how the helpdesk takes care of clients and this requires a modification to the database, I need to be very mindful that I don't damage components of the schema made use by various other services. This situation typically results in needing a big quantity of regression testing.

Secondly, consumers are connected to a specific innovation choice, probably now it makes good sense to save customers in a relational data source, so my customers utilize an ideal (possibly DB-specific) driver to speak to it. What happens if with time we recognize we would be better off storing information in a nonrelational database? Can it make that decision? consumers are intimately connected to the implementation of the customer support. As we reviewed earlier, we really wish to ensure that application detail is concealed from customers to enable our solution a level of freedom in terms of how it changes its internals with time. Farewell, loose coupling.

Let's believe about actions for a minute. There is mosting likely to be reasoning connected with how a consumer is altered. Where is that reasoning? If customers are directly controlling the DB, after that they have to own the associated reasoning. The reasoning to execute the same types of manipulation to a client may now be spread out amongst numerous consumers. If the storage facility, enrollment UI, and also call center UI all require to edit customer details, I require to take care of a bug or alter the habits in three various locations, and even deploy those adjustments too Goodbye, communication.

Keep in mind when we discussed the core concepts behind great microservices? Strong cohesion as well as loose combining with data source combination, we lose both points. Data source combination makes it simple for solutions to share information, yet does nothing regarding sharing actions. Our internal depiction is revealed over the cable to our customers, as well as it can be tough to prevent making breaking changes, which inevitably brings about a worry of any change in all. Avoid at (nearly) all costs.

For the remainder of the phase, we'll explore different designs of assimilation that entail working together services, which themselves conceal their very own inner representations.

## Concurrent Versus Asynchronous.

Before we start diving right into the specifics of various technology options, we need to talk about among the most vital choices we can make in terms of just how solutions collaborate.

Should communication be asynchronous or simultaneous? This essential selection indeed guides us towards specific execution detail, with synchronous interaction, a call is made to a remote server, which obstructs until the procedure finishes. With asynchronous communication, the customer does not await the procedure to finish before returning, and also might not care whether or not the procedure completes at all.

Synchronous communication can be less complicated to reason about. We understand when points have completed effectively or not. Asynchronous communication can be extremely helpful for longrunning tasks, where maintaining a connection open for an extended period of time in between the client and web server is impractical. It also works extremely well when you require reduced latency, were obstructing a phone call while waiting for the outcome can reduce things down. Because of the nature of mobile networks and also tools, firing off demands and presuming points have actually worked (unless told otherwise) can make sure that the UI stays responsive even if the network is highly laggy. On the flipside, the innovation to take care of asynchronous communication can be a bit much more engaged, as we'll discuss shortly.

These 2 various settings of communication can allow 2 different idiomatic styles cooperation: request/response or event-based, ith request/response, a customer initiates a demand and waits for the reply. This model clearly straightens well to synchronous interaction, but can work for asynchronous communication as well. I could begin an procedure and sign up a callback, asking the server to allow me recognize when my procedure has finished.

With an event-based cooperation, we invert points. Rather than a client starting demands requesting for things to be done, it rather states this point happened and anticipates various other events to understand what to do. We never ever tell anyone else what to do. Event-based systems by their nature are asynchronous. The smarts are much more equally dispersed that is, the company reasoning is not centralized into core minds, but rather pushed out extra equally to the numerous partners. Event-based cooperation is additionally highly decoupled. The customer that sends out an occasion doesn't have any kind of way of understanding that or what will certainly respond to it, which also suggests that you can include new customers to these occasions without the client ever requiring to know.

So exist any kind of other vehicle drivers that might push us to select one design over another? One important aspect to take into consideration is how well these designs are fit for resolving an often complex trouble: just how do we take care of processes that cover solution boundaries and might be future?

## Orchestration Versus Choreography

As we begin to model an increasing number of complex reasoning, we need to deal with the trouble of handling service procedures that extend across the border of individual solutions. As well as with microservices, we'll hit this restriction earlier than normal. Let's take an instance from MusicCorp, and also consider what takes place when we produce a consumer:

1. A new document is produced in the loyalty points bank for the customer.
2. Our postal system sends out a welcome pack.
3. We send a welcome e-mail to the client.

When it involves actually implementing this circulation, there are two designs of style we can adhere to. With orchestration, we rely upon a main brain to overview and also drive the procedure, much like the conductor in an orchestra. With choreography, we inform each component of the system of its job, as well as allow it exercise the information, like professional dancers all finding their way and reacting to others around them in a ballet.

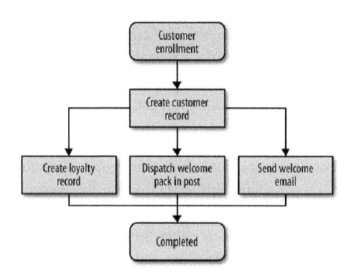

Let's consider what an orchestration service would certainly resemble for this circulation. Here, most likely the easiest point to do would be to have our customer support serve as the central mind. On creation, it speaks with the loyalty factors financial institution, email service, and also postal service as we see in Figure through a collection of request/response calls. The customer service itself can after that track where a customer is in this procedure. It can examine to see if the consumer's account has actually been set up, or the email sent. We obtain to take the flowchart in Figure and version it straight into code. We could also utilize tooling that executes this for us, probably using an appropriate rules engine. Business devices exist for this very function in the type of organisation procedure modeling software. Assuming we make use of concurrent request/response, we can also understand if each stage has functioned.

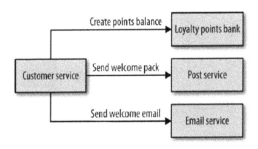

The downside to this orchestration approach is that the customer care can end up being also a lot of a main regulating authority. It can come to be the hub in the center of a web, as well as a central factor where logic starts to live. I have seen this approach lead to a handful of clever "god" solutions telling anemic CRUD-based solutions what to do.

With a choreographed approach, we might rather just have the client service emit an event in an asynchronous manner, claiming Customer produced.

The e-mail solution, postal solution, as well as commitment factors financial institution after that just register for these events and respond as necessary, as in Figure above.This strategy is substantially a lot more decoupled. , if some other solution needed to reach to the creation of a client, it simply needs to subscribe to the events and when required, do its task. The disadvantage is that the specific view of the company procedure we see in Figure is now only unconditionally reflected in our system.

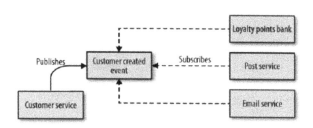

This means extra work is needed to make sure that you can monitor as well asa  track that the right things have actually taken place. Would you know if the loyalty points bank had a bug insect for some reason factor set up the correct right? One approach I like for dealing with this is to construct a tracking system that clearly matches the sight of the business procedure in the Figure but then tracks what each of the solutions does as independent entities, letting you see strange exceptions mapped onto the extra specific procedure circulation. The flowchart we saw earlier isn't the driving force, however simply one lens whereby we can see exactly how the system is behaving.

As a whole, I have discovered that systems that have a tendency more towards the choreographed method are more freely combined, and are a lot more adaptable and open to transform. You do require to.

do additional job to check and track the procedures across system borders, nonetheless. I have actually found most greatly managed executions to be extremely breakable, with a greater cost of modification. With that said in mind, I strongly like going for a choreographed system, where each service is clever enough to understand its function in the whole dancing.

There are numerous aspects to unload below. Synchronous phone calls are simpler, and we reach know if points worked straightaway. If we like the semiotics of request/response but are taking care of longer-lived procedures, we could just initiate asynchronous demands as well as wait for callbacks. On the other hand, asynchronous event cooperation assists us adopt a choreographed technique, which can produce significantly a lot more decoupled services something we intend to pursue to ensure our services are individually releasable.

We are, naturally, totally free to blend and also match. Some modern technologies will certainly fit more normally into one design or another. We do, however, need to value some of the different technological implementation information that will certainly additionally aid us make the right call. To begin with, let's check out two innovations that fit well when we are thinking about request/response: remote procedure telephone call (RPC) and REpresentational State Transfer.

# CHAPTER FIVE

## R.E.S.T

Representational State Transfer (REMAINDER) is a building style inspired by the Internet. There are numerous concepts and restrictions behind the REST style, but we are most likely When we deal with assimilation difficulties in a microservices, focus on those that really assist our globe, and also when we're looking for a different design to RPC for our solution interfaces.

Most important is the concept of sources. You can consider a resource as a point that the service itself finds out about, like a Customer. The web server creates different depictions of this Client on demand.

How a source is shown on the surface is entirely decoupled from just how it is stored internally. A client might request for a JSON representation of a Client, as an example, even if it is kept in a completely different layout. When a client has a depiction of this Customer, it can after that make requests to alter it, as well as the server may or may not follow them.

There are several styles of REST, and I touch only briefly on them here. I strongly advise you have a look at the Richardson Maturity Model, where the different designs of REST are compared.

REMAINDER itself does not actually chat about underlying protocols, although it is most frequently used over HTTP. I have seen applications of REST making use of really different protocols in the past, such as serial or USB, although this can need a great deal of job. A few of the features that HTTP offers us as part of the requirements, such as verbs, make executing REST over HTTP much easier, whereas with other methods you'll have to manage these attributes yourself.

REMAINDER and HTTP.

HTTP itself specifies some valuable abilities that play very well with the REST design. For example, the HTTP verbs (e.g., GET, POST, as well as PUT) already have well-understood significances in the HTTP spec regarding how they should deal with resources. The REMAINDER architectural design really tells us that methods ought to behave similarly on all sources, as well as the HTTP specification happens to specify a number of techniques we can utilize.

OBTAIN: it obtains a resource in an idempotent means, and also POST creates a new resource. This.

methods we can stay clear of whole lots of different createCustomer or editCustomer techniques. Instead, we can simply POST a client representation to demand that the server develop a new resource, and start a GET demand to recover a representation of a source.

Conceptually, there is one endpoint in the type of a customer source in these situations, as well as the operations we can execute upon it are baked into the HTTP protocol. HTTP also brings a huge environment of sustaining tools as well as modern technology. We reach make use of HTTP caching proxies like Varnish as well as tons balancers like mod_proxy, and lots of surveillance tools currently have great deals of assistance for HTTP out of the box. These building blocks allow us to handle big volumes of HTTP website traffic and path them wisely, in a rather precise method. We also reach use all the offered security controls with HTTP to safeguard our interactions. From basic auth to customer certs, the HTTP community provides us whole lots of devices to make the safety and security process much easier, that claimed, to get these benefits, you need to utilize HTTP well. Utilize it badly, and also it can be as insecure as well as hard to scale as any other innovation out there. Use it right, however, and you obtain a great deal of assistance.

Keep in mind that HTTP can be made use of to apply RPC as well. SOAP, as an example, obtains routed over. HTTP, however makes use of extremely little of the requirements. Verbs are neglected, as are basic points like HTTP error codes. All frequently, it appears, the existing, well-understood standards and innovation are neglected in support of brand-new requirements that can only be applied making use of brand-new technology conveniently offered by the very same firms that aid develop the brand-new criteria in the very first location!

Hypermedia As the Engine of Application State.

One more principle introduced in REST that can assist us prevent the combining between the customer and also servers is the concept of hypermedia as the engine of application state (commonly abbreviated as HATEOAS, as well as boy, did it need an acronym). This is relatively thick phrasing as well as a fairly intriguing concept, so let's damage it down a little bit.

Hypermedia is an idea where a piece of content consists of links to different other pieces of material in a variety of layouts (e.g., message, pictures, appears). This need to be rather acquainted to you, as it's what the average websites does: you comply with links, which are a type of hypermedia controls, to see related content. The suggestion behind HATEOAS is that clients ought to execute communications (possibly bring about state shifts) with the web server by means of these web links to various other resources. It does not need to know where precisely clients live on the web server by knowing which URI to strike; instead, the client seeks and navigates web links to discover what it needs.

This is a little bit of a strange idea, so let's initial step back and think about exactly how people connect with a websites, which we've already established is rich with hypermedia controls. Believe of the Amazon buying website, the place of the shopping cart has actually altered over time. The graphic has altered. The web link has transformed. However as human beings we are wise enough to see a buying cart still, understand what it is, and connect with it. We have an understanding of what a shopping cart indicates, also if the precise form as well as underlying control utilized to represent it has actually transformed. We understand that if we wish to watch the cart, this is the control we wish to engage with. This is why internet pages can change incrementally over time. As long as these implied contracts between the client as well as the site are still satisfied, adjustments do not require to be damaging changes.

With hypermedia controls, we are trying to achieve the same level of smarts for our digital consumers. Let's take a look at a hypermedia control that we might have for MusicCorp. We've accessed a source standing for a magazine entrance for a provided album in.

Example 4-2. In addition to info concerning the cd, we see a variety of hypermedia controls Hypermedia used on a cd listing.

<album>

<name>Offer Blood</name>

<link rel="/artist" href="/artist/theBrakes" />

<description>

Incredible, short, brutish, amusing and loud. Should buy!

</description>

<linkrel="/instantpurchase"href="/instantPurchase/234" />

</album>

< link rel ="/ instantpurchase" href ="/ instantPurchase/1234"/ > This hypermedia control

reveals us where to discover information about the musician.

As well as if we desire to buy the cd, we currently know where to go JSON, XML, or Another Thing.

Making use of typical textual formats offers clients a great deal of flexibility as to exactly how they consume resources, and also REMAINDER over HTTP allows us utilize a variety of layouts. The instances I have actually given up until now made use of XML, however at this phase, JSON is a lot more preferred web content kind for solutions that persuade HTTP.

The truth that JSON is a much simpler format indicates that usage is additionally less complicated. When compared to XML as another winning, supporters likewise mention its loved one density aspect, although this isn't frequently a real-world issue.

JSON does have some downsides, though. XML specifies the web link control we made use of previously as a hypermedia control. The JSON standard doesn't specify anything comparable, so internal styles are regularly utilized to shoe-horn this principle in the Hypertext Application.

Language (HAL) attempts to repair this by defining some typical requirements for hyperlinking for JSON (and also XML too, although perhaps XML needs less help). , if you follow the HAL criterion, you can make use of tools like the online HAL web browser for exploring hypermedia controls, which can make the job of creating a customer much simpler.

We aren't restricted to these 2 layouts, obviously. We can send out virtually anything over HTTP if we want, also binary. I am seeing an increasing number of individuals just making use of HTML as a style as opposed to XML. For some user interfaces, the HTML can do double obligation as a UI as well as an API, although there are challenges to be avoided right here, as the interactions of a human and also a computer are fairly different! It is absolutely an eye-catching idea. There are great deals of HTML Parsers out there.

Personally, though, I am still a fan of XML. Some of the device assistance is much better. For instance, if I wish to extract just particular components of the payload (a strategy we'll review a lot more in "Versioning") I can make use of XPATH, which is a well-understood requirement with great deals of tool support, or perhaps CSS selectors, which several locate also less complicated. With JSON, I have JSONPATH, however this is not widely sustained. Due to the fact that, I find it strange that individuals choose JSON.

it is light-weight and also great, after that attempt and push ideas into it like hypermedia controls that already exist in XML. I accept, however, that I am possibly in the minority below as well as that JSON is the style of choice for most individuals!.

## Downsides to REMAINDER Over HTTP

In terms of convenience of consumption, you can not conveniently create a customer stub for your REMAINDER over HTTP application method like you can with RPC. Sure, the truth that HTTP is being used indicates that you reach make the most of all the excellent HTTP client collections out there, yet if you want to make use of as well as implement hypermedia controls as a client you are quite a lot on your own. Directly, I believe customer libraries can do much far better at this than they do, and they are absolutely better now than in the past, yet I have actually seen this apparent boosted complexity cause individuals backsliding into smuggling RPC over HTTP or developing shared client libraries. Shared code in between client as well as web server can be really harmful, as we'll discuss in "DRY and also the Perils of Code Reuse in a Microservice World".

An even more technicality is that some web server structures do not actually support all the HTTP verbs well. That implies that it might be very easy for you to create a trainer for OBTAIN or POST demands, however you might have to leap with hoops to get PUT or ERASE demands to function. Proper REMAINDER structures like Jacket do not have this trouble, and also you can typically work about this, yet if you are secured into certain structure options this might limit what style of REST you can use.

Performance may additionally be a problem. REST over HTTP hauls can really be much more Portable than SOAP because it sustains alternative styles like JSON or even binary it will still be nowhere near as lean a binary method as Thrift may be. The expenses of HTTP for each request may also be an issue for low-latency demands.

HTTP, while it can be fit well to big volumes of website traffic, isn't fantastic for low-latency When contrasted to alternative protocols that are constructed on top of, interactions. Transmission Control Protocol (TCP) or various other networking technology. In spite of the name, WebSockets, as an example, has very little to do with the Web. After the initial HTTP handshake, it's just a TCP link in between customer as well as web server, however it can be a much extra reliable means for you to stream data for a web browser. If this is something you're interested in, note that you aren't really using a lot of HTTP, let alone anything to do with REST.

For server-to-server communications, if very reduced latency or little message dimension is important, HTTP communications in general might not be a great suggestion. You may require to choose various underlying protocols, like User Datagram Protocol (UDP), to achieve the efficiency you want, and numerous RPC frameworks will quite happily work on top of networking procedures aside from TCP. Consumption of the hauls themselves requires even more job than is provided by some RPC implementations that sustain sophisticated serialization and also deserialization devices.

These can end up being a combining point in their own right between client and also server, as applying forgiving visitors is a nontrivial activity (we'll discuss this quickly), yet from the factor of sight of standing up and running, they can be really eye-catching.

Regardless of these downsides, REST over HTTP is a reasonable default selection for service-toservice communications. If you wish to know much more, I recommend REST in Practice (O'Reilly), which covers the topic of REST over HTTP extensive.

**Complexities of Asynchronous Architectures.**

Some of this asynchronous things appears fun, right? Event-driven architectures appear to lead to dramatically much more decoupled, scalable systems. And also they can. These shows designs do result in a rise in intricacy. This isn't simply the intricacy called for to manage publishing as well as subscribing to messages as we just talked about, however additionally in the other problems we may face. When taking into consideration long-running async request/response, we need to assume about what to do when the response returns. Does. it returned to the exact same node that started the demand? If so, what if that node is down? If not, do I need to save info somewhere so I can react appropriately? Short-lived async can be easier to handle if you've got the ideal APIs, but however, it is a different means of believing for programmers who are accustomed to intra-process concurrent message phone calls.

Time for a sign of things to come. Back in 2006, I was servicing constructing a pricing system for a financial institution. We would certainly check out market occasions, and also function out which things in a profile required to be repriced. When we established the listing of points to overcome, we placed these all onto a message line up. We were making usage of a grid to produce a swimming pool of pricing workers, permitting us to scale backwards and forwards the prices ranch on demand. These employees made use of the contending consumer pattern, each one gobbling messages as rapid as feasible until there was nothing entrusted to process.

The system was up as well as running, and we were feeling instead smug. One day, however, just after we pushed a release out, we struck an unpleasant issue, our employees kept passing away.

Ultimately, we found the problem. A pest had slipped in wherein a certain kind of pricing request would certainly create an employee to crash. We were making use of a transacted line up as the worker died, its lock on the request break, and also the prices request was returned on the queue just for one more worker to choose it up as well as pass away. This was a traditional example of what Martin Fowler calls a tragic failover.

Apart from the bug itself, we would certainly fell short to specify an optimum retry limit for the work on the line. We repaired the pest itself, as well as also set up an optimum retry. Yet we likewise recognized. we required a means to see, and potentially replay, these poor messages. We finished up having to carry out a message medical facility (or dead letter line), where messages got sent if they fallen short. If required, we also created a UI to watch those messages and retry them. These kinds of issues aren't promptly obvious if you are only aware of simultaneous pointto-point communication.

The associated intricacy with event-driven designs and asynchronous shows in general leads me to think that you should beware in exactly how excitedly you start adopting these suggestions. Guarantee you have great tracking in location, as well as strongly consider the usage of correlation IDs, which permit you to map requests throughout process.

limits, as we'll cover extensive in Chapter 8.

I also highly suggest Enterprise Combination Patterns (Addison-Wesley), which has a whole lot more detail on the various programs patterns that you may require toconsider in this room.

# CHAPTER SIX

## DRY AND THE PERILS OF CODE REUSE IN A MICROSERVICE

One of the phrases we programmers hear a lot is DRY: Its interpretation is sometimes streamlined as attempting to avoid replicating code, DRY more accurately suggests that we wish to prevent replicating our system actions and expertise. This is extremely reasonable recommendations in general, Having great deals of lines of code that do the very same point makes your codebase larger than needed, and as a result more difficult to reason about. When you intend to alter habits, which actions is copied in several components of your system, it is very easy to fail to remember almost everywhere you require to make a change, which can lead to pests. Utilizing DRY as a concept, in basic, makes good sense. DRY is what leads us to produce code that can be recycled. We pull duplicated code right into abstractions that we can after that call from multiple areas. Perhaps we go as far as making a shared library that we can make use of almost everywhere! This approach, nevertheless, can be stealthily harmful in a microservice architecture.

Among the things we wish to stay clear of in all costs is overly coupling a microservice and customers such that any tiny modification to the microservice itself can create unnecessary changes to the consumer. In some cases, nevertheless, the usage of shared code can create this extremely combining. At one client we had a library of typical domain name things that represented the core entities in operation in our system. This library was made use of by all the services we had. When a change was made to one of them, all solutions had actually to be updated. Our system communicated through message lines up, which also needed to be drained pipes of their currently void components, and also problem betide you if you failed to remember.

If your use common code ever before leaks outside your solution limit, you have actually presented a possible kind of combining. Using typical code like logging collections is great, as they are inner concepts that are invisible to the outdoors. RealEstate takes advantage of a customized service design template to help bootstrap brand-new solution creation. As opposed to make this code shared, the company duplicates it for every brand-new service to guarantee that coupling doesn't leak in. My basic general rule: do not violate DRY within a microservice, however be relaxed around violating DRY across all services. The evils of as well much coupling between services are far worse than the issues created by code duplication. There is one specific usage case well worth checking out even more

Customer Libraries.

I've talked with greater than one group who has firmly insisted that creating customer libraries for your solutions is a crucial component of developing solutions in the first place. The debate is that this makes it easy to use your service, and stays clear of the duplication of code needed to eat the service itself.

The problem, obviously, is that if the exact same people produce both the web server API as well as the customer. API, there is the threat that logic that should exist on the web server begins leaking right into the customer. I need to recognize: I've done this myself. The even more logic that slips right into the client library, the a lot more communication begins to break down, and you find yourself having to change numerous clients to roll out repairs to your server. You also restrict innovation selections, If you mandate that the customer collection has to be made use of, especially. A version for client collections I such as is the one for Amazon Web Services (AWS). The underlying SOAP or REST web service calls can be made straight, yet everyone ends up using simply among the numerous software program advancement kits (SDKs) that exist, which provide abstractions over the underlying API. These SDKs, though, are created by the neighborhood or AWS individuals aside from those who work with the API itself. This degree of splitting up appears to work, and also stays clear of several of the challenges of client libraries as part of the reason.

When the upgrade happens, works so well is that the client is in cost of. If you drop the course of customer collections yourself, see to it this holds true.

Netflix in specific locations unique focus on the customer library, but I stress that people view that totally with the lens of staying clear of code duplication. In fact, the customer libraries made use of by Netflix are as much (if not more) about guaranteeing integrity and also scalability of their systems. The Netflix client collections handle service discovery, failing modes, logging, and also other facets that aren't really concerning the nature of the service itself. Without these shared customers, it would be tough to guarantee that each piece of client/server communications behaved well at the huge range at which Netflix runs. Their use at Netflix has definitely made it easy to stand up and also running as well as boosted performance while likewise making sure the system acts well. According to at least one individual at

Netflix, in time this has actually caused a degree of coupling between customer and also server that has actually been bothersome.

If the client collection approach is something you're considering, it can be important to separate out customer code to manage the underlying transport procedure, which can take care of things like service discovery and also failure, from points connected to the location solution itself. Decide whether you are mosting likely to demand the customer library being made use of, or if you'll permit individuals making use of different innovation heaps to make telephone calls to the underlying API.

And finally, make sure that the customers supervise of when to upgrade their client libraries: we require to ensure we preserve the ability to launch our solutions independently of each other!

# CHAPTER SEVEN

## VERSIONING

One versioning remedy typically cited is to have various variations of the service live at once, and for older consumers to path their web traffic to the older version, with more recent versions seeing the new one, as received. This is the method utilized sparingly by Netflix in scenarios where the cost of altering older customers is too expensive, particularly in rare situations where tradition devices are still connected to older versions of the API. Personally, I am not a fan of this suggestion, and also comprehend why Netflix uses it hardly ever. If I need to fix an internal insect in my service, I currently need to repair and release 2 different collections of services.

This would probably indicate I have to branch the codebase for my service, as well as this is constantly troublesome. Second, it means I need smarts to take care of directing consumers to the Microservice. This habits certainly winds up being in middleware someplace or several nginx scripts, making it more challenging to reason concerning the actions of the system.

Lastly, take into consideration any relentless state our service may handle. Customers developed by either variation of the solution need to be kept and also made noticeable to all services, no matter which version was made use of to develop the data in the very first area. This can be an added source of intricacy

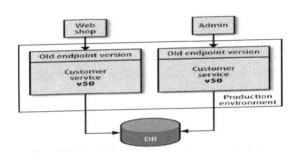

Coexisting simultaneous service versions for a short time period can make best sense, when you're doing things like canary launches or blue/green implementations. In these situations, we may be existing together variations only for a couple of mins or possibly hrs, and also normally will have only 2 different variations of the solution present at the same time. The longer it takes for you to get consumers updated to the more recent version as well as launched, the a lot more you must seek to exist together different endpoints in the exact same microservice instead of exist together totally different variations. I remain unsure that this job is beneficial for the ordinary task.

Customer Interfaces.

Thus far, we have not truly touched on the globe of the individual interface. A few of you around may simply be offering a chilly, hard, clinical API to your consumers, but numerous of us locate ourselves wanting to produce beautiful, useful customer interfaces that will certainly thrill our customers. Yet we actually do require to consider them in the context of combination. The user interface, after all, is where we'll be pulling all these microservices together right into something that makes good sense to our customers.

In the past, when I first started computing, we were primarily discussing large, fat clients that operated on our desktop computers. I invested lots of hrs with Motif and after that Swing trying to make my software as wonderful to use as feasible. Commonly these systems were simply for the creation and control of regional documents, however numerous of them had a server-side element. My initial job at thought Works entailed creating a Swing-based digital point-of-sale system that was just part of a great deal of moving components, the majority of which were on the web server.

After that came the Web. We started considering our UIs as being thin rather, with even more reasoning on the web server side. At first, our server-side programs provided the whole page and sent it to the client web browser, which did very little. Any communications were managed on the web server side, through POSTs and gets caused by the individual clicking on links or loading in forms.

With time, JavaScript became a more preferred choice to add dynamic actions to the browser-based UI, and some applications could now be suggested to be as fat as the old desktop computer clients.

Restrictions.

Restrictions are the different types in which our users communicate with our system. On a desktop computer web application, for instance, we consider restraints such as what browser site visitors are making use of, or their resolution. However mobile has actually brought a whole host of new constraints. The means our mobile applications interact with the server can have an impact. It isn't simply regarding pure bandwidth worries, where the constraints of mobile networks can play a part. Different kind of communications can drain battery life, leading to some go across consumers.

The nature of interactions modifications, also. I can not easily right-click on a tablet computer. On a mobile phone, I might want to create my interface to be utilized primarily one-handed, with a lot of procedures being regulated by a thumb. Elsewhere, I might allow people to connect with services through SMS in position where data transfer is at a premium the usage of SMS as an interface is massive in the global south.

Although our core solutions our core offering could be the exact same, we need a means to adapt them for the various restraints that exist for every kind of interface. When we consider different designs of interface composition, we need to make sure that they resolve this obstacle. Allow's check out a few designs of interface to see exactly how this could be achieved.

# CHAPTER EIGHT

## API COMPOSITION

Thinking that our solutions currently speak XML or JSON per other through HTTP, an apparent choice readily available to us is to have our interface interact straight with these APIs, as in Figure 4-7. An online UI might use JavaScript GET demands to recover information, or POST demands to transform it. Also for native mobile applications, initiating HTTP communications is rather straightforward. The UI would then need to develop the numerous elements that make up the interface, dealing with synchronization of state and also the like with the web server. This if we were making use of a binary protocol for service-to-service communication would certainly be more difficult for online customers, yet might be fine for indigenous mobile phones.

There are a number of downsides with this approach. First, we have little capacity to tailor the feedbacks for various type of tools. When I obtain a consumer document, do I require to pull back just the same data for a mobile store as I do for a helpdesk application? One remedy to this approach is to enable customers to define what areas to draw back when they make a demand, however this thinks that each solution supports this type of communication.

An additional essential inquiry: that produces the individual interface? Individuals who take care of the solutions are removed from just how their solutions are emerged to the individuals-- for instance, if one more group is developing the UI, we can be drifting back into the bad old days of split style where making also tiny changes calls for modification demands to several groups.

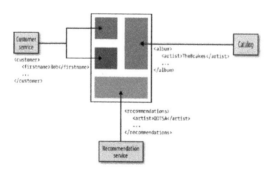

This communication could likewise be fairly chatty. Opening lots of phone calls straight to solutions can be fairly extensive for mobile devices, as well as could be an extremely inefficient use a client's mobile strategy!

Having an API entrance can help below, as you can reveal calls that aggregate multiple underlying calls, although that itself can have some disadvantages that we'll discover quickly.

## UI Fragment Composition.

Instead of having our UI make API telephone calls and also map everything back to UI controls, we might have our services provide parts of the UI directly, as well as after that just pull these fragments in to develop a UI, as in Figure 4-8. Think of, for example, that the recommendation service offers a recommendation widget that is integrated with various other controls or UI fragments to produce a general UI. It could get rendered as a box on a websites in addition to various other content.

A variant of this technique that can function well is to assemble a collection of coarser-grained parts of a UI. Rather than producing small widgets, you are setting up whole panes of a thick client application, or perhaps a set collection pages for a websiteInternet site. These coarser-grained fragments are offered up from server-side applications that are in turn making the proper API telephone calls. When the pieces line up well to, this design functions best team ownership. Maybe the team that looks after order administration in the songs store provides all the web pages connected with order monitoring.

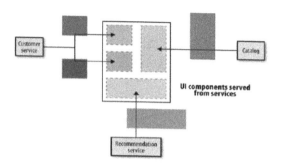

Services straight dishing out UI parts for assembly. You still require some type of assembly layer to draw these parts with each other. This can be as basic as some server-side templating, or, where each collection of web pages comes from a different app, probably you'll need some smart URI directing.

Among the crucial advantages of this approach is that the same group that makes adjustments to the services can also supervise of making modifications to those components of the UI. It enables us to get modifications out much faster. There are some troubles with this strategy. Making sure consistency of the user experience is something we require to resolve. Users intend to have a seamless experience, not to feel that various parts of the user interface job in various methods, or offer a different layout language. There are techniques to avoid this problem, however, such as living style guides, where possessions like HTML parts, CSS, as well as photos can be shared to help provide some level of uniformity.

One more probem is harder to deal with. What occurs with native applications or thick customers? We can't dish out UI components. We might use a hybrid technique and utilize indigenous applications to dish out HTML parts, yet this technique has actually been revealed time as well as once more to have downsides. So if you need a native experience, we will need to fall back to a technique where the frontend application makes API phone calls and deals with the UI itself. However, also if we think about web-only UIs, we still might want extremely different therapies for different types of gadgets. Structure receptive elements can help, naturally.

There is one essential trouble with this strategy that I'm unsure can be addressed. In some cases the capacities provided by a service do not fit neatly into a widget or a page. Certain, I might wish to surface area referrals in a box on a page on our web site, however suppose I wish to weave in vibrant recommendations in other places? I desire the kind ahead to when I browse automatically set off fresh suggestions, for instance. The more cross-cutting a kind of interaction is, the much less most likely this design will fit and also the extra likely it is that we'll fall back to just making API calls.

**Backends for Frontends.**

A typical solution to the trouble of chatty interfaces with backend services, or the demand to differ content for various kinds of devices, is to have a server-side aggregation endpoint, or API entrance. This can marshal numerous backend telephone calls, differ as well as aggregate content if required for various devices, and offer it up.

When these server-side endpoints come to be thick layers with, this method lead to disaster excessive habits. They end up getting handled by different teams, and being another place where reasoning needs to alter whenever some capability changes.

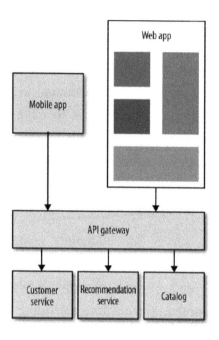

The trouble that can happen is that generally we'll have one gigantic layer for all our solutions. This results in every little thing being thrown in together, and suddenly we begin to lose seclusion of our numerous interface, limiting our capability to release them separately. A design I like which I've seen work well is to restrict using these backends to one specific interface or application.

This pattern is sometimes described as backends for frontends (BFFs). It enables the groupfocusing on any offered UI to additionally manage its own server-side parts. You can see these backends as components of the customer interface that happen to be installed in the web server.

Some kinds of UI might need a marginal server-side footprint, while others might need a whole lot a lot more. This can rest between our if you require an API verification as well as authorization layer. BFFs and also our UIs.

The risk with this method coincides similar to any type of accumulating layer; it can tackle reasoning it shouldn't. The business reasoning for the various capacities these backends make use of ought to remain in the solutions themselves. These BFFs should only include habits particular to providing a particular user experience.

# CHAPTER NINE

## TESTING MICROSERVICES

The world of automated screening has actually progressed significantly since I initially started writing code, and each month there appears to be some new tool or method to make it even better. However challenges stay as how to properly as well as efficiently examine our capability when it spans a dispersed system. This phase breaks down the issues connected with testing finer-grained systems and also offers some services to help you ensure you can launch your new capability with self-confidence.

Checking covers a lot of ground. Also when we are simply discussing automated tests, there are a lot to think about. With microservices, we have actually included one more degree of complexity. Understanding what various sorts of tests we can run is essential to aid us balance the sometimes-opposing forces of getting our software application into production as swiftly as feasible versus ensuring our software is of sufficient high quality.

**Kinds of Tests**

As an expert, I like pulling out the odd quadrant as a method of categorizing the globe, and also I was starting to stress this publication would not have one. Thankfully, Brian Marick generated a wonderful categorization system for examinations that fits right in. Figure 7-1 shows a variant of Marick's quadrant from Lisa Crispin and Janet Gregory's book Agile Testing (Addison-.Wesley) that aids classify the various kinds of tests.

At the base, we have examinations that are technology-facing that is, tests that aid the developers in developing the system to begin with efficiency tests and small-scoped device examines come under this classification all commonly automated. This is compared to the top half of the quadrant, where tests aid the nontechnical stakeholders comprehend how your system works. These could be large-scoped, end-to-end examinations, as displayed in the top-left.

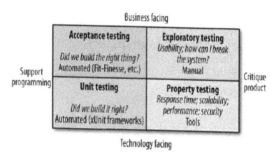

Acceptance Test square, or manual screening as typified by customer screening done versus a UAT system, as displayed in the Exploratory Testing square.

Each sort of test received this quadrant has a location. Precisely just how much of each test you desire to do will depend upon the nature of your system, yet the bottom line to understand is that you have numerous choices in terms of how to test your system. The fad recently has been away from any kind of large-scale hands-on testing, in favor of automating as long as feasible, and I certainly agree with this technique. If you presently accomplish huge quantities of manual screening, I would certainly suggest you deal with that before continuing also much down the path of microservices, as you will not obtain most of their benefits if you are incapable to verify your software application swiftly and effectively.

For the objectives of this phase, we will certainly neglect manual screening. Although this type of testing can be really valuable and certainly has its part to play, the distinctions with testing a microservice design mainly play out in the context of various kinds of automated examinations, to make sure that is where we will certainly concentrate our time.

However when it pertains to automated tests, the number of each examination do we want? An additional design will be available in really useful to assist us address this question, and comprehend what the various trade-offs might be.

Examination Scope.

Test Pyramid aid to describe what kinds of automated tests you require. The pyramid helps us consider the ranges the examinations ought to cover, however also the percentages of various types of tests we need to go for Cohn's initial design split automated examinations right into Unit, Service, and also UI, which you can see in Figure below.

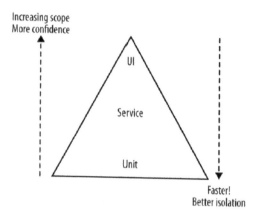

The trouble with this design is that all these terms imply different points to various individuals. "Service" is specifically strained, and there are numerous interpretations of a device examination out there. Is an examination a device test if I only examine one line of code? I would certainly state yes. Is it still an unit examination if I test several functions or classes? I 'd say no, but lots of would disagree! I have a tendency to stick with the Unit and also Service names in spite of their obscurity, however much prefer calling UI tests end-to-end examinations, which we'll do from currently on, state the challenge, it's worth us checking out what these different layers indicate.

Allow's take a look at a functioned instance. In the figure we have our helpdesk application as well as our main internet site, both of which are engaging with our customer care to get, examine, and edit customer details. Our client solution subsequently is talking to our loyalty factors financial institution, where our clients accumulate factors by getting Justin Bieber CDs. Most likely. This is obviously a bit of our general music shop system, yet it is an adequate piece for us to study a couple of different situations we may want to test

System Examinations.

These are examinations that commonly test a solitary feature or approach telephone call. The tests created as a negative effects of test-driven design (TDD) will certainly drop right into this classification, as do the types of tests produced by techniques such as property-based screening. We're not introducing solutions here, and also are limiting the use of outside data or network connections. In general, you desire amultitude of these kind of examinations. Done right, they are extremely, extremely quickly, as well as on modern-day hardware you can anticipate to run many hundreds of these in much less than a minute.

These are examinations that aid us developers therefore would be technology-facing, not businessfacing, in Marick's terminology. They are likewise where we want to catch the majority of our insects.

So, in our instance, when we think of the client service, system examinations would cover tiny parts of the code alone. The prime objective of these tests is to give us really quickly feedback concerning whether our performance is excellent. Tests can be essential to support refactoring of code, permitting us to restructure our code as we go, recognizing that our small-scoped examinations will certainly catch us if we make an error.

Solution Examinations.

Solution examinations are developed to bypass the interface and test services directly. In a monolithic application, we may just be testing a collection of courses that give a service to the UI. For a system comprising a number of services, a solution examination would certainly test a private solution's capabilities.

The reason we desire to check a solitary service by itself is to enhance the seclusion of the examination to make searching for and repairing problems much faster. To accomplish this seclusion, we need to stub out all external partners so just the service itself remains in scope, as in the Figure below.

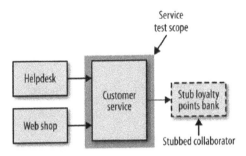

A few of these examinations can be as quickly as small tests, however if you choose to check against an actual data source, or look at networks to stubbed downstream collaborators, examination times can boost. They also cover more range than an easy unit examination, so that when they fail it can be harder to detect what is broken than with a device examination. Nonetheless, they have much less relocating parts as well as are therefore less weak than larger-scoped tests.

End-to-End Tests

End-to-end examinations are tests run against your entire system. Frequently they will be driving a GUI

via a web browser, but can quickly be imitating various other type of user interaction, like posting a data.

These tests cover a whole lot of manufacturing code, as we see in Figure 7-6. So when they pass, you really feel great: you have a high degree of self-confidence that the code being examined will certainly function in manufacturing. Yet this boosted scope features disadvantages, and also as we'll see shortly,they can be really complicated to do well in a microservices context. Extent of end-to-end examinations on our instance system

Trade-Offs

When you're reading the pyramid, the crucial point to take away is that as you increase the pyramid, the test scope rises, as does our self-confidence that the capability being tested jobs. On the other hand, the comments cycle time boosts as the examinations take much longer to run, and also when a test fails it can be more challenging to determine which functionality has broken.

As you drop the pyramid, generally the examinations come to be much faster, so we obtain a lot faster responses cycles. We discover damaged functionality much faster, our continual combination builds are faster, and we are much less most likely to carry on to a brand-new task prior to discovering we have actually damaged something. When those smaller-scoped examinations stop working, we likewise often tend to recognize what broke, typically precisely what line of code. On the flipside, we do not obtain a great deal of self-confidence that our system in its entirety jobs if we've only examined one line of code!

When broader-scoped tests like our service or end-to-end examinations fail, we will certainly attempt to compose a quick device test to catch that problem in the future. Because means, we are continuously attempting to boost our comments cycles.

Basically every team I've worked with has actually utilized different names than the ones that Cohn uses in the pyramid. Whatever you call them, the key takeaway is that you will want tests of various range for various objectives.

Exactly how Many?

If these tests all have compromises, how numerous of each type do you want? A good policy of thumb is that you most likely desire an order of size more examinations as you descend the pyramid, but the crucial thing is recognizing that you do have various types of automated.

If your current balance gives you an issue, examinations and also recognizing! I serviced one monolithic system, for example, where we had 4,000 system tests, 1,000 solution tests, as well as 60 end-to-end examinations. We made a decision that from a feedback point of view we had method too lots of service and end-to-end examinations (the latter of which were the worst culprits in affecting feedback loops), so we worked hard to change the test insurance coverage with smaller-scoped tests.

A typical anti-pattern is what is commonly referred to as an examination snow cone, or inverted pyramid. Here, there are little to no small-scoped tests, with all the protection in largescoped examinations. These tasks frequently have glacially sluggish examination runs, as well as extremely long feedback cycles. If these examinations are run as part of constant combination, you will not get numerous builds, and also the nature of the develop times implies that the develop can remain broken for a lengthy duration when something does break.

Implementing Service Tests.

Executing device tests is a relatively simple affair in the grand plan of points, and there is lots of documentation available discussing how to write them. The service as well as end-toend tests are the ones that are extra fascinating.

Our solution tests wish to check a slice of performance across the whole service, however to separate ourselves from various other services we require to discover some means to stub out every one of our collaborators. If we wanted to write a test like this for the consumer solution from, we would certainly deploy an instance of the client service, and also as gone over previously we would intend to stub out any kind of downstream solutions.

Among the initial points our continual integration develop will do is create a binary artefact for our solution, so deploying that is quite uncomplicated. But just how do we manage fabricating the downstream collaborators?

Our service test collection needs to launch stub solutions for any downstream partners (or ensure they are running), as well as set up the service under examination to link to the stub services. After that we require to set up the stubs to send out actions back to mimic the real-world services. We might configure the stub for the commitment factors bank to return recognized factors equilibriums for sure customers.

Stubbing or buffooning.

I mean that we produce a stub service when I chat regarding stubbing downstream collaborators that respond with tinned reactions to well-known requests from the service under test. For instance I could inform my stub factors bank that when asked for the balance of customer 123, it needs to return 15,000. If the stub is called 0, 1, or 100 times, the examination doesn't care.

A variation on this is to use a mock as opposed to a stub.

When using a simulated, I actually go even more as well as make sure the telephone call was made. If the anticipated telephone call is not made, the examination fails. Executing this technique needs even more smarts in the fake partners that we develop, as well as if excessive used can trigger tests to come to be breakable. As noted, nevertheless, a stub does not care if it is called 0, 1, or sometimes. In some cases, however, buffoons can be extremely useful to make sure that the anticipated side impacts take place. I may want to check that when I develop a customer, a brand-new points equilibrium is established for that consumer. The equilibrium between stubbing as well as mocking phone calls is a delicate one, and is simply as stuffed in solution examinations as in device examinations. As a whole, though, I use stubs even more than mocks for solution tests.

Generally, I rarely make use of buffoons for this kind of screening. Yet having a device that can do both is.

Valuable. While I feel that stubs and also mocks are preferably well separated, I recognize the difference can be misleading to some, especially when some people toss in various other terms like counterfeits, spies, as well as dummies. Martin Fowler calls every one of these things, including stubs as well as mocks, test increases.

## A Smarter Stub Service.

Usually for stub solutions I've rolled them myself. I've utilized everything from Apache or Nginx to embedded Jetty containers and even command-line-launched Python web servers made use of to launch stub web servers for such test cases. I've most likely duplicated the very same work time and time once again in producing these stubs. My ThoughtWorks colleague has actually possibly conserved a lot of us a portion of job with his stub/mock webserver called Mountebank.

You can assume of Mountebank as a small software home appliance that is programmable by means of HTTP. The reality that it occurs to be written in NodeJS is completely opaque to any calling solution. When it introduces, you send it commands informing it what port to stub on, what method to take care of (currently TCP, HTTP, and also HTTPS are sustained, with even more planned), as well as what responses it must send when demands are sent. It additionally supports.

If you want to use it as a mock, establishing expectations. You can remove these stub or include endpoints at will, making it feasible for a single

Mountebank circumstances to stub even more than one downstream reliance.

If we desire to run our solution examinations for simply our customer service we can launch the customer support, and also a Mountebank instance that serves as our loyalty factors bank. And if those tests pass, I can deploy the consumer solution straightaway! Or can I? What about the solutions that call the customer support-- the helpdesk and also the internet shop? If, do we recognize we have made a modification that may break them? Certainly, we have forgotten the vital tests on top of the pyramid: the end-to-end examinations.

**Tricky End-to-End Tests.**

In a microservice system, the capabilities we reveal through our user interfaces are delivered by a number of solutions. The point of the end-to-end examinations as detailed in Mike Cohn's pyramid is to drive functionality through these interface versus everything below to offer us a review of a big quantity of our system. To execute an end-to-end examination we need to release numerous services with each other, after that run an examination versus all of them. Obviously, this test has a lot more extent, resulting in extra confidence that our system works! On the various other hand, these tests are responsible to be slower and also make it tougher to diagnose failing. Allow's dig into them a bit a lot more utilizing our previous example to see how these examinations can suit.

Imagine we wish to press out a new variation of the client service. We intend to deploy our modifications right into production immediately, but are concerned that we may have introduced a modification that might damage either the web or the helpdesk shop. No problem, let's deploy all of our solutions together, as well as run some tests against the helpdesk and also web shop to see if we've presented a bug. Now an ignorant method would be to simply include these examinations onto completion of our customer support pipeline, Including our end-to-end tests stage: the appropriate strategy?

Much, so good. Yet the first concern we have to ask ourselves is which version of the various other solutions should we utilize? Should we run our tests versus the versions of helpdesk as well as internet store that remain in manufacturing? It's a sensible assumption, but what happens if there is a brand-new variation of either the helpdesk or internet store queued up to go online; what should we do after that?

Another issue: if wc have a set of customer support tests that deploy great deals of solutions and run examinations versus them, what concerning the end-to-end examinations that the other services run? , if they are testing the same point, we might discover ourselves covering lots of the same ground, and also may duplicate a great deal of the initiative to deploy all those solutions in the first area.

We can deal with both of these problems elegantly by having numerous pipes fan in to a solitary, end-to-end examination phase. Below, whenever a brand-new construct of among our solutions is caused, we run our end-to-end examinations, Some CI devices with far better construct pipe support will certainly allow fan-in versions like this out of the package. A standard way to handle end-to-end inspections throughout solutions.

Any time of the modifications of our services, we run the tests local to that solution. , if those examinations pass, we trigger our assimilation tests. Great, eh? Well, there are a few issues.

Checking After Production

A lot of screening is done before the system remains in production. With our examinations, we are specifying a collection of versions with which we wish to prove whether our system works as well as behaves as we would like, both functionally as well as nonfunctionally. Yet if our versions are not best, we will certainly come across troubles when our systems are utilized in anger. Bugs slip into manufacturing, brand-new failure modes are uncovered, and our customers utilize the system in ways we could never ever anticipate.

One reaction to this is commonly to specify increasingly more examinations, and improve our designs, to catch much more concerns early and also lower the variety of troubles we encounter with our running production system. At a specific factor we have to accept that we hit diminishing returns with this technique. With screening before implementation, we can not reduce the opportunity of failure to absolutely no.

**Separating Deployment from Release.**

One way in which we can capture much more problems prior to they occur is to prolong where we run our examinations past the conventional predeployment actions. Rather, if we can deploy our software, as well as test it sitting prior to guiding production tons against it, we can identify concerns certain to a given setting. A typical instance of this is the smoke test collection, a collection of tests designed to be run versus newly deployed software application to validate that the release worked. These tests assist you gct any neighborhood environmental problems. , if you're utilizing a solitary command-line command to release any type of provided microservice (and also you need to), this command needs to run the smoke tests automatically.

An additional example of this is what is called blue/green deployment. With blue/green, we have two duplicates of our software program released at once, but just one version of it is getting real requests.

Let's think about a straightforward example, In production, we have v123 of the customer support live. We wish to release a brand-new version, v456. We release this together with v123, but do not route any type of web traffic to it. Instead, we carry out some testing in situ versus the recently deployed version. As soon as the tests have functioned, we guide the production tons to the new v456 variation of the customer support. It is common to keep the old variation around for a brief duration of time, enabling for a rapid backup if you identify any mistakes.

Number 7-12. Utilizing blue/green releases to different implementation from release. Executing blue/green release calls for a couple of points. One needs to be able to direct production website traffic to various hosts (or collections of hosts). You can do this by transforming DNS entries, or updating load-balancing arrangement. You also need to be able.

Once, to provision sufficient organizes to have both variations of the microservice running at. If you're utilizing a flexible cloud company, this can be simple. Making use of blue/green implementations permits you to lower the danger of deployment, along with gives you the chance to change ought to you experience an issue. The whole process can be if you obtain excellent at this entirely automated, with either the full roll-out or go back happening without any type of human intervention.

Fairly besides the advantage of allowing us to test our solutions sitting before sending them production website traffic, by keeping the old variation running while we do our launch we considerably decrease the downtime associated with launching our software application. Relying on what system is made use of to carry out the traffic redirection, the switchover between.

variations can be entirely invisible to the client, giving us zero-downtime implementations.

There is another method worth going over briefly right here too, which is in some cases confused with blue/green releases, as it can make use of a few of the exact same technological executions. It is called a canary launching.

Canary Launching.

With canary releasing, we are confirming our newly released software by routing quantities of manufacturing website traffic against the system to view if it performs as anticipated." Doing as expected" can cover a variety of things, both useful as well as nonfunctional. As an example, we might check that a freshly released service is responding to requests within 500ms, or that we see the same symmetrical mistake prices from the brand-new and also the old solution. However you might go deeper than that. Imagine we have actually launched a brand-new variation of the referral solution. We could run both of them side by side yet see if the recommendations produced by the brand-new version of the solution lead to as numerous expected sales, seeing to it that we have not released a suboptimal algorithm.

You get to return swiftly if the brand-new launch is negative. You can press enhancing if it is excellent quantities of web traffic via the brand-new variation. Canary launching differs from blue/green in that you can expect versions to exist together for longer, and you'll usually vary the quantities of website traffic.

Netflix uses this strategy extensively. Prior to launch, brand-new solution versions are released together with a baseline cluster that stands for the exact same version as production. Netflix then runs a part of the production lots over a variety of hours versus both the new version as well as the baseline, scoring both. The firm then continues to a full if the canary passes roll-out right into production.

When considering canary releasing, you need to choose if you are mosting likely to divert a part of production requests to the canary or simply copy manufacturing load. Some teams have the ability to shadow manufacturing web traffic and direct it to their canary. This way, the existing production and also canary variations can see specifically the exact same demands, but only the results of the production demands are seen externally. This allows you to do a side-by-side comparison while removing the opportunity that a consumer request can see a failing in the canary.

The job to shadow manufacturing traffic can be complex, however, especially if the events/requests being repeated aren't idempotent. Canary launching is an effective strategy, and can aid you confirm brand-new variations of your software with actual web traffic, while providing you devices to take care of the risk of pushing out a bad launch. It does require an extra complex arrangement, however, than blue/green deployment, and a bit more believed.

You could anticipate to exist side-by-side various versions of your services for longer than with blue/green, so you might be connecting up more equipment for longer than previously. You'll additionally require much more advanced traffic directing, as you may intend to increase or down the portions of the traffic to obtain even more self-confidence that your launch works. , if you already.

Take care of blue/green implementations, you may have some of the foundation already..

# CHAPTER TEN

## MONITORING MICROSERVICES

As I've ideally shown thus far, damaging our system up right into smaller, fine-grained microservices cause several benefits. It additionally, nevertheless, adds complexity when it pertains to checking the system in production. In this chapter, we'll check out the difficulties related to monitoring and also recognizing problems in our fine-grained systems, and I'll detail some of things you can do to have your cake and eat it too!

It's a silent Friday afternoon, and also the group is looking forward to sloping. off early to the club as a means to begin a weekend break away from work. After that instantly the. emails get here. The website is being mischievous! Twitter is ablaze with your company's failings, your manager is eating your ear off, and also the leads of a quiet weekend break disappear.

What's the initial point you need to recognize? What the heck has gone incorrect?

In the globe of the monolithic application, we at the very least have an extremely obvious place to start.

Site slow down? Web site providing weird mistakes?

CPU at 100%? Well, you obtain the idea. Having a single solitary factor failure failing makes failure failing somewhat simplerLess complex Currently allow's think of our very own, microservice-based system. The abilities we use our users are offered from several small solutions, a few of which interact with yet even more services to accomplish their jobs. There are lots of advantages to such a method.

( which is great, as or else this book would be a waste of time), yet in the world of monitoring, we have an extra complicated issue on our hands.

We now have numerous servers to monitor, numerous logfiles to filter with, and numerous. locations where network latency could trigger issues. Just how do we approach this? We require to make sense of what otherwise could be a chaotic, tangled mes the last point any one of us intends to deal with on a Friday afternoon (or at any type of time, concerned that!).

The solution right here is quite uncomplicated: check the small points, and also make use of gathering to see the bigger picture. To see how, we'll begin with the most basic system we can: a single node.

Solitary Service, Single Server.

one host, running one solution. Currently we need to check it in order to recognize when something fails so we can repair it. So what should we try to find?

A single service on a single host.

We'll want to monitor the host itself. CPU, memory every one of these things are beneficial.

We'll need to know what they need to be when points are healthy, so we can notify when they head out of bounds. We can utilize if we want to run our very own tracking software application something like Nagios to do so, otherwise use a hosted service fresh Relic. Next off, we'll desire to have access to the logs from the web server itself. If a customer reports a mistake,.

When as well as where the error is, these logs must pick it up and ideally inform us. At this point, with our solitary host we can most likely manage with just going to the host and also. using command-line tools to check the log. We might also get progressed as well as make use of logrotate to move old logs out of the way as well as prevent them taking up all our disk area.

Lastly, we might intend to keep an eye on the application itself. At a bare minimum, surveillance the response time of the service is a great suggestion. You'll possibly have the ability to do this by checking out the logs coming either from a web server fronting your solution, or possibly from the service itself. If we obtain very innovative, we may wish to track the number of errors we are reporting.

Time passes, lots raise, as well as we find ourselves needing to scale .

# CHAPTER ELEVEN

## CASCADE

Cascading failings can be specifically treacherous. Imagine a scenario where the network connection between our songs store site and the directory service drops. The solutions themselves show up healthy and balanced, yet they can not talk with each other. , if we just looked at the health and wellness of the private service, we wouldn't know there is a problem. Using synthetic surveillance-- as an example, to simulate a customer browsing for a song would get the issue. Yet we 'd additionally need to report on the fact that one service can not see an additional in order to figure out the reason for the issue.

As a result, keeping an eye on the combination points between systems is vital. Each service circumstances needs to reveal the health and wellness as well as track of its downstream dependencies, from the data source to various other teaming up services. You ought to additionally permit this information to be accumulated to provide you a rolled-up photo. You'll desire to see the reaction time of the downstream calls, If it is erroring, as well as additionally discover.

you can make use of libraries to carry out a circuit breaker around network phones call to aid you take care of plunging failures in a much more classy fashion, enabling you to even more beautifully deteriorate your system. Several of these collections, such as Hystrix for the JVM, also do a great work of providing these checking capacities for you.

Standardization

As we've covered previously, among the continuous balancing acts you'll need to manage is where to permit for decisions to be made directly for a solitary solution versus where you require to standardize throughout your system. In my point of view, tracking is one location where standardization is extremely important. With services collaborating in great deals of different means to supply capacities to individuals using numerous interfaces, you need to watch the system in an all natural means.

You must attempt to write your logs out in a standard layout. You absolutely wish to have all your metrics in one area, and you might wish to have a checklist of basic names for your metrics also; it would certainly be extremely bothersome for one service to have actually a statistics called ResponseTime, and also an additional to have actually one called RspTimeSecs, when they imply the same point. As always with standardization, devices can assist, As I've said before, the secret is making It simple the ideal point-- so why not give preconfigured online maker photos with logstash and collectd all set to go, in addition to application collections that let you speak with.

Consider the Audience

All this information we are collecting is for a purpose. More particularly, we are gathering all this data for various people to assist them do their tasks; this data becomes a phone call to activity.

Several of this information requires to cause an immediate contact us to activity for our support group for instance, when it comes to one of our synthetic monitoring tests stopping working. Various other data, like the fact that our CPU load has actually raised by 2% over the recently, is possibly only of interest when we're doing capacity preparation. Your boss is most likely going to would like to know today that income dipped 25% after the last release, yet possibly doesn't need to be woken up since look for "Justin Bieber" have risen 5% in the last hour. When, what our individuals want to react and also see to right now is different than what they require piercing down. So, for the kind of person who will certainly be taking a look at this data, consider the adhering to:

- What they require to know now
- What they might want later on
- How they such as to consume information
- Alert on things they need to recognize now.

Develop large noticeable display screens with this details that sit in the edge of the area. Provide simple access to the data they require to understand later on. And also hang around with them to understand how they intend to eat data. A conversation regarding all the subtleties included in the graphical display screen of quantitative info is certainly outside the scope of this publication, but a great area to begin is Stephen.

The Future.

I have seen lots of organizations where metrics are siloed into various systems Application-level metrics, like the variety of orders positioned, wind up in a proprietary analytics system like Omniture, which is commonly offered just to pick parts of the service, or else finishes up in the dreadful data warehouse, aka where information goes to pass away.

Coverage from such systems is frequently not offered in real time, although that is starting to adjustment. System metrics like action times, mistake prices, as well as CPU tons are stored in systems that the procedures groups can access. These systems normally permit real-time reporting, as typically the point of them is to prompt an immediate phone call to action.

Historically, the suggestion that we can discover vital business metrics a day or more later on was great, as normally we were unable to respond fast sufficient to this information to do anything about it anyway. Currently, however, we operate in a world in which a lot of us can and do push out multiple launches daily. Groups now measure themselves not in terms of the number of factors they complete, but rather maximize for how much time it takes for code to get from laptop computer to live. In such a setting, we require all our metrics at our fingertips to take the right action. Paradoxically, the extremely systems that store business metrics are commonly not tuned for prompt accessibility to information, yet our operational systems are.

Why take care of operational and also service metrics in the very same means? Inevitably, both types of points break down to occasions that state something occurred at X. So, if we can link the systems we utilize to gather, accumulation, and store these events, and make them available for reporting, we end up with a much less complex style.

Riemann is an occasion web server that permits relatively sophisticated aggregation and also directing of events and also can form component of such an option. Suro is Netflix's information pipeline and also operates in a comparable space. Suro is explicitly used to manage both metrics linked with individual behavior, and also extra functional data like application logs. This data can after that be dispatched to a variety of systems, like Storm for real-time analysis, Hadoop for offline set handling, or Kibana for log analysis.

Many companies are relocating a fundamentally various instructions: away from having specialized device chains for different sorts of metrics as well as towards more generic event routing systems qualified of substantial scale. These systems handle to provide a lot more flexibility, while at the same time really streamlining our architecture.

# CHAPTER TWELVE

## MICROSERVICES SECURITY

We've ended up being acquainted with stories regarding safety breaches of large-scale systems causing our information being revealed to all kind of dodgy personalities. Extra lately, occasions like the Edward Snowden revelations have made us even more aware of the worth of information that business hold about us, as well as the value of data that we hold for our customers in the systems we build. This chapter will give a brief introduction of some elements of security you should take into consideration when developing your systems. While not meant to be extensive, it will certainly set out several of the primary choices available to you and give you a beginning factor for your own more research study.

We need to think of what security our information needs while in transportation from one factor to another, and what security it needs at remainder. We need to consider the safety and security of our underlying running systems, and also our networks as well. There is so much to believe around, and also Much we could do! So just how much security do we require? Just how can we exercise what is sufficient safety?

We also need to assume of the human component. How do we understand who a person is, and what he can do? And also exactly how does this connect to exactly how our servers speak with each various other? Let's begin there.

Verification and Authorization.

Authentication as well as authorization are core principles when it involves individuals and things that interact with our system. In the context of security, authentication is the process by which we confirm that an event is that she claims she is. For a human, you generally verify an individual by having her kind in her username and also password. We presume that only she has access to this info, and consequently that the person entering this details have to be her. Other, a lot more complicated systems exist also, naturally. My phone currently allows me utilize my finger print to confirm that I am who I say I am. Normally, when we're talking abstractly regarding who or what is being verified, we describe that party as the principal.

Permission is the device by which we map from a principal to the action we are permitting her to do. Frequently, when a principal is verified, we will be provided info about her that will certainly assist us choose what we should let her do. We might, for example, be told what department or workplace she operates in-- items of details that our systems can use to choose what she can and also can refrain from doing.

For single, monolithic applications, it is common for the application itself to handle verification as well as authorization for you. Django, the Python web framework, comes out of the box with user administration. when it comes to distributed systems.

We require to believe of even more innovative systems. We don't want everyone to have to log in individually for various systems, using a different username as well as password for every, as soon as, the goal is to have a solitary identity that we can confirm.

**Usual Single Sign-On Implementations.**

A typical technique to verification and consent is to use some kind of solitary signon ( SSO) service. SAML, which is the ruling application in the enterprise area, and also OpenID Connect both offer capabilities in this field. Essentially they utilize the exact same core concepts, although the terminology differs slightly. The terms used here are from SAML.

When a major attempts to access a source (like an online interface), she is routed to validate with an identification supplier. This may ask her to provide a username and also password, or could make use of something much more progressed like two-factor authentication. When the identification provider is pleased that the principal has actually been confirmed, it gives info to the company, permitting it to make a decision whether to grant her access to the resource.

This identification provider can be an externally hosted system, or something inside your own organization. Google, for instance, gives an OpenID Connect identity carrier. For business, though, it is typical to have your own identification supplier, which may be connected to your firm's directory site service. A directory service could be something like the Light-weight Directory Access Protocol (LDAP) or Active Directory. These systems permit you to store info regarding principals, such as what functions they play in the organization Often, the directory service and also the identity company are identical, while sometimes they are different however linked. Okta, for instance, is a held SAML identity provider that handles jobs like two-factor authentication, but can link to your firm's directory site solutions as the source of truth. SAML is a SOAP-based criterion, and is understood for being fairly intricate to collaborate with despite the libraries and also tooling offered to sustain it. OpenID Connect is a criterion that has emerged as a details execution of OAuth 2.0, based upon the means Google and others manage SSO. It uses easier REST phone calls, as well as in my point of view is likely to make inroads right into enterprises due to its improved convenience of use. Its largest road block right now is the lack of identification service providers that support it. For a public-facing web site, you might be OK making use of Google as your provider, but for internal systems or systems where you desire much more control over and presence into just how and where your information is installed, you'll desire. your own internal identification supplier. At the time of composing, OpenAM and also Gluu are 2 of the really few choices offered in this room, contrasted to a wealth of choices for SAML ( including Active Directory, which seems to be almost everywhere). Until as well as unless existing identity service providers begin sustaining OpenID Connect, its growth may be limited to those situations where people more than happy making use of a public identification company.

So while I think OpenID Connect is the future, it's fairly possible it'll take a while to get to extensive fostering.

**Solitary Sign-On Gateway.**

Within a microservice setup, each service could make a decision to manage the redirection to, as well as handshaking with, the identification carrier. Undoubtedly, this can mean a great deal of duplicated job. A shared collection can help, however we 'd have to be cautious to prevent the coupling that can originate from shared code. This likewise wouldn't help if you had numerous various.

Technology Heaps.

As opposed to having each service handle handshaking with your identification service provider, you can utilize an entrance to function as a proxy, resting between your solutions and the outdoors. The suggestion is that we can systematize the behavior for redirecting the user and also execute the handshake in just one location making use of a portal to handle SSO.

However, we still need to solve the problem of just how the downstream solution receives info regarding principals, such as their username or what roles they play. , if you're utilizing HTTP, it could occupy headers with this information. Shibboleth is one tool that can do this for you, and also I've seen it made use of with Apache to excellent effect to deal with combination with SAML-based identity providers.

Another trouble is that if we have made a decision to unload duty for verification to a gateway, it can be tougher to reason regarding exactly how a microservice acts when taking a look at it alone. Make sure your if you go the gateway path programmers can launch their solutions behind one without as well much work.

One last trouble with this technique is that it can time-out you right into a false complacency. I like the idea of protection detailed-- from network border, to subnet, to firewall program, to device, to running system, to the underlying equipment. You have the capability to execute security steps at all of these points, several of which we'll obtain into soon. I have actually seen some people put all their eggs in one basket, depending on the portal to deal with every step for them. When we have a single point of, and we all know what happens failure .

Obviously you might use this gateway to do other things. , if making use of a layer of Apache circumstances running Shibboleth, as an example, you could additionally decide to terminate HTTPS at this level, run breach detection, as well as so on. Do be mindful. Portal layers often tend to tackle more and extra performance, which itself can wind up being a gigantic combining factor. And also the even more capability something has, the greater the assault surface.

Fine-Grained Authorization.

A portal may have the ability to offer rather reliable grainy verification. For example, it could stop accessibility to any non-logged-in individual to the helpdesk application. Presuming our entrance can extract features concerning the principal as a result of the authentication, it may be able to make even more nuanced decisions. For instance, it is usual to put individuals in groups, or assign them to duties. We can use this information to comprehend what they can do. For the helpdesk application, we might enable access just.

to principals with a particular function (e.g., STAFF). Beyond allowing (or forbiding) access to specific sources or endpoints, however, we need to leave the rest to the microservice itself; it will need to make more decisions concerning what procedures to enable.

Back to our helpdesk application: do we enable any team member to see any as well as all details? More probable, we'll have various duties at the workplace. For instance, a principal in the CALL_CENTER team may be enabled to view any type of piece of details regarding a consumcr except his repayment details. The principal could also be able to release reimbursements that quantity could be capped. A person who has the CALL_CENTER_TEAM_LEADER duty, however, might be able to release bigger refunds. These decisions need to be regional to the microservice concerned. I have seen individuals use the various features supplied by identity carriers in horrible ways, making use of truly finegrained duties like CALL_CENTER_50_DOLLAR_REFUND, where they wind up putting info certain to one part of among our system's behavior right into their directory site solutions. This is a nightmare to preserve and offers extremely little extent for our solutions to have their own independent lifecycle, as suddenly a chunk of details regarding how a solution acts lives elsewhere, probably in a system taken care of by a different part of the company.

Rather, prefer grainy duties, designed around just how your organization functions. Going completely back to the early phases, keep in mind that we are developing software application to match how our organization functions. Use your roles in this means too.

# CHAPTER THIRTEEN

## SERVICE-TO-SERVICE AUTHENTICATION AND AUTHORIZATION

Up to this factor we've been making use of the term principal to describe anything that can be and also verify authorized to do points, but our examples have really been around humans making use of computer systems. Yet what concerning programs, or various other solutions, verifying with each various other?

Allow Everything Inside the Perimeter

Our initial option can be to just presume that any phone call to a service made from inside our boundary are implicitly relied on. Relying on the level of sensitivity of the data, this might be great. Some companies try to guarantee protection at the boundary of their networks, as well as therefore assume they do not need to do anything else when two solutions are chatting with each other. However, needs to an assaulter permeate your network, you will certainly have little defense against a common man-in-the-middle assault. If the enemy determines to obstruct and check out the information being sent, change the data without you understanding, or even in some conditions claim to be the thing you are talking with, you may not understand much concerning it.

This is without a doubt the most common kind of inside-perimeter depend on I see in organizations. They might decide to run this traffic over HTTPS, however they do not do much else. I'm not claiming that is an advantage! For the majority of the organizations I see utilizing this design, I fret that the implicit trust design is not an aware decision, however more that individuals are not aware of the risks to begin with.

HTTP( S) Basic Authentication

HTTP Basic Authentication permits a client to send a username and password in a common HTTP header. The server can then examine these information as well as verify that the client is enabled to access the solution. The advantage below is that this is an incredibly wellunderstood and well-supported method. The issue is that doing this over HTTP is extremely bothersome, as the username as well as password are not sent in a secure manner. Any kind of intermediate event can consider the details in the header and see the data. Therefore, HTTP.

Fundamental Authentication ought to usually be used over HTTPS. When utilizing HTTPS, the client gains strong guarantees that the web server it is speaking with is who the client believes it is. It likewise gives us additional defense against people eavesdropping on the website traffic between the client as well as web server or tinkering the haul.

The web server requires to manage its own SSL certifications, which can become bothersome when it is handling several machines. Some organizations tackle their own certification releasing procedure, which is an extra management and also operational concern. Tools around handling this in an automatic style are nowhere near as mature as they could be, and it isn't simply the releasing process you need to handle. Self-signed certificates are not conveniently revokable, and therefore call for a lot much more assumed around calamity situations. See if you can dodge all this job by staying clear of self-signing altogether. One more drawback is that traffic sent out using SSL can not be cached by reverse proxies like.

Varnish or Squid.

This means that if you need to cache traffic, it will certainly have to be done either inside the server or inside the customer. You can fix this by having a tons balancer terminate the SSL web traffic, and also having the cache sit behind the load balancer. We also need to consider what happens if we are using an existing SSO solution, like SAML, that already has accessibility to usernames and passwords. Do we desire our standard service auth to utilize the very same set of credentials, permitting us one procedure for revoking and also issuing them? We might do this by having the solution speak to the exact same directory service that backs our SSO service. We could keep the passwords and also usernames ourselves inside the service, however after that we run the threat of duplicating habits.

One note: in this approach, all the server recognizes is that the client has the username and also password. If this info is coming from a machine we expect; it, we have no idea could be originating from any person on our network.

Use SAML or OpenID Connect, if you are already using SAML or OpenID Connect as your authentication as well as permission system, you can simply use that for service-to-service interactions also. , if You're making use of an entrance, you'll need to course all in-network traffic using the entrance too. This approach should just function out of the if each solution is dealing with the assimilation itself box. The advantage below is that you're utilizing existing framework, and get to streamline all your service accessibility controls in a main directory web server. We would certainly still require to If we wanted to stay clear of man-in-the-middle assaults, path this over HTTPS.

Customers have a set of credentials they use to verify themselves with the identity company, and the service obtains the information it needs to choose any type of fine-grained authentication.

This does imply you'll need a make up your customers, sometimes described as a service account. Numerous organizations utilize this method rather commonly. A word of caution, though: if you are going to develop service accounts, attempt to maintain their use narrow. So consider each microservice having its own collection of qualifications. This makes revoking/changing gain access to easier if the credentials end up being compromised, as you just require to revoke the collection of qualifications that have been affected.

There are a couple of other drawbacks. Initially, simply as with Basic Auth, we need to securely store our credentials: where do the username as well as password live? The customer will. need to find some protected way to save this information. The various other problem is that some of the innovation in this area to do the verification is rather tedious to code for. SAML, in specific, makes implementing a client an unpleasant affair. OpenID Connect has a simpler operations, yet as we discussed earlier it isn't that well supported yet.

Client Certificates.

Another technique to confirm the identity of a customer is to utilize capabilities in Transport Layer Security (TLS), the follower to SSL, in the form of client certificates.

Below, each client has an X. 509 certificate mounted that is utilized to establish a link between client as well as server. The web server can verify the authenticity of the customer certification, supplying solid assurances that the customer stands. The functional challenges right here in certification management are much more burdensome than with simply using server-side certifications. It isn't just some of the basic problems of creating as well as handling a majority of certificates; rather, it's that with all the complexities around the certificates themselves, you can anticipate to spend a great deal of time trying to detect why a service will not approve what you believe to be a totally valid customer certificate. And also after that we have to consider the trouble of withdrawing and reissuing certifications ought to the most awful take place. Using wildcard certificates can aid, but will not address all issues. This extra problem implies you'll be looking to utilize this strategy when you are particularly worried regarding the sensitivity of the information being sent out, or if you are sending data using networks you do not completely control. So you could decide to protect interaction of extremely essential data. Between parties that is sent out over the Internet.

HMAC Over HTTP.

As we talked about earlier, using Basic Authentication over plain HTTP is not extremely. If we are fretted concerning the username and password being compromised, practical. The conventional alternative is course web traffic HTTPS, yet there are some disadvantages. Other than handling the certificates, the overhead of HTTPS web traffic can position additional strain on servers (although, to be sincere, this has a reduced influence than it did a number of years ago), and also the website traffic can not easily be cached.

An alternate technique, as used thoroughly by Amazon's S3 APIs for AWS and partially of the OAuth requirements, is to utilize a hash-based messaging code (HMAC) to authorize the request.

With HMAC the body demand together with a private key is hashed, and the resulting hash is sent together with the request. The web server then utilizes its own copy of the exclusive key and also the demand body to re-create the hash. It permits the demand if it matches.

The nice point right here is that if a guy between tinker the demand, after that the hash will not match as well as the web server knows the request has actually been damaged. And also the personal secret is never sent in the request, so it can not be endangered in transit! The included benefit is that this traffic can then more conveniently be cached, and also the overhead of generating the hashes might well be reduced than dealing with HTTPS web traffic (although your gas mileage might differ).

There are three disadvantages to this approach. First, both the client and web server require a shared trick that requires to be communicated somehow. How do they share it? It might be hardcoded at both ends, however after that you have the problem of withdrawing access if the secret becomes endangered. If you communicate this secret over some different procedure, after that you need to ensure that protocol is likewise extremely secure!

Second, this is a pattern, not a requirement, and also hence there are different means of applying it. Because of this, there is a scarcity of great, open, as well as useful implementations of this strategy. As a whole, if this method interests you, then do some even more reading to understand the various means it is done. I would certainly go as much as to claim simply look at exactly how Amazon does this for S3 as well as duplicate its method, specifically using a reasonable hashing function with a accordingly lengthy key like SHA-256. JSON internet symbols (JWT) are likewise worth considering, as they apply an extremely comparable approach and also appear to be getting grip. Yet understand the trouble of getting this stuff right. My coworker was collaborating with a team that was. executing its very own JWT application, left out a solitary Boolean check, as well as invalidated its entire verification code! Hopefully in time we'll see even more multiple-use library applications.

Comprehend that this approach makes sure only that no third celebration has adjusted the demand which the private essential itself stays personal. The remainder of the data in the demand will still show up to celebrations snooping on the network.

API Keys.

All public APIs from services like Twitter, Google, Flickr, and also AWS utilize API keys. API keys allow a solution to identify who is telephoning, and also location restrictions on what they can do. Frequently the limitations go past merely admitting to a resource, and can expand to actions like rate-limiting specific callers to shield top quality of solution for various other people.

When it involves utilizing API keys to manage your very own microservice-to-microservice method, the exact mechanics of how it works will certainly rely on the technology you use. Some systems make use of a single API trick that is shared, and make use of an approach similar to HMAC as just defined. An even more typical technique is to make use of a personal and public vital set.Commonly, you'll take care of secrets centrally, just as we would certainly take care of identifications of people centrally. The entrance model is incredibly popular in this room.

Part of their popularity originates from the fact that API keys are focused on simplicity of use for programs. Compared to taking care of a SAML handshake, API trick-- based verification is much less complex as well as much more uncomplicated.

The precise capacities of the systems differ, and also you have numerous options in both the open and industrial resource area. Some of the items simply manage the API secret exchange as well as some fundamental crucial management. Various other devices provide whatever up to and also including rate restricting, money making, API directories, and discovery systems.

Some API systems allow you to connect API tricks to existing directory solutions. This would certainly enable you to issue API secrets to principals (representing systems or people) in your company, as well as manage the lifecycle of those type in the same method you would certainly handle their regular qualifications. This opens up the opportunity of enabling accessibility to your solutions in various means but maintaining the exact same resource of fact-- as an example, making use of SAML to authenticate people for SSO, and using API tricks for service-to-service communication,.

as received Figure.

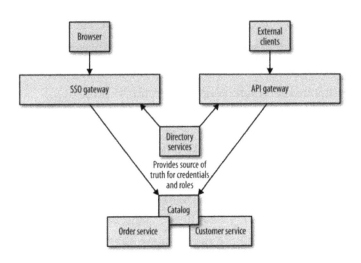

Service Ownership

What do I suggest by service possession? Generally, it suggests that the team possessing a service is accountable for making modifications to that solution. The group needs to feel free to restructure the code nevertheless it desires, as long as that change does not break consuming solutions. For

lots of teams, possession encompasses all aspects of the solution, from sourcing requirements to building, deploying, and preserving the application. This version is particularly prevalent with microservices, where it is much easier for a little group to have a tiny service. This enhanced degree of possession brings about boosted autonomy and also speed of distribution. Having one team responsible for preserving the application and releasing suggests it has an reward to produce  services that are simple to release; that is, concerns about "throwing something over the wall" dissipate when there is nobody to throw it to!

This design is absolutely one I prefer. It pushes the choices to individuals best able to make them, giving the group both boosted power and autonomy, however additionally making it responsible for its work. I've seen much too many developers hand their system over for screening or deployment stages as well as think that their work is done then.

Motorists for Shared Services.

I have actually seen several groups adopt a version of common solution possession. I discover this strategy suboptimal, for factors currently reviewed. The chauffeurs that create individuals to choose shared solutions are very important to recognize, especially as we may be able to discover some compelling different models that can address people's underlying concerns.

Too Hard to Split.

Clearly, among the factors you may find on your own with a single service had by more than one team is that the price of splitting the solution is too expensive, or possibly your organization may not see the point of it. This is an usual event with huge monolithic systems. I wish some of the suggestions if this is the primary obstacle you encounter. You could additionally consider combining teams with each other, to align a lot more carefully with the design itself.

Attribute Teams.

The idea of function teams (aka feature-based groups) is that a tiny group drives the development of a set of features, carrying out all performance called for also if it cuts throughout component (or perhaps service) boundaries. The goals of attribute teams are sensible sufficient. This framework enables the team to preserve a concentrate on the end outcome and guarantees that the job is joined up, avoiding several of the obstacles of trying to coordinate changes throughout several various teams.

In several circumstances, the attribute team is a reaction to standard IT organizations where group structure is lined up around technical boundaries. You may have a team that is responsible for the UI, another one more is responsible liable the application logic, andAs well as a third managing the database. In this atmosphere, a feature group is a substantial step up, as it functions throughout all these layers to supply the functionality. With wholesale adoption of attribute groups, all solutions can be considered shared. Everyone can transform every solution, every item of code. The role of the service custodians below becomes much more complicated, if the role exists at all. Sadly, I seldom see operating custodians whatsoever where this pattern is taken on, bring about the sorts of concerns we gone over earlier.

But let's once again consider what microservices are: services modeled after an organisation domain name, not a technical one. And also if our group that owns any provided service is in a similar way lined up along the service domain, it is much extra likely that the team will certainly be able to preserve a client emphasis, as well as see even more of the feature growth via, since it has a holistic understanding and also possession of all the technology connected with a service.

Cross-cutting adjustments can happen, obviously, however their probability is significantly decreased by our avoiding technology-oriented groups.

Distribution Bottlenecks.

One crucial factor individuals relocate towards common solutions is to stay clear of delivery traffic jams. What if there is a big stockpile of modifications that need to be made in a solitary service? Let's think of that we are presenting the ability for a customer to see the category of a track throughout our products, as well as adding a an all new sort of supply: virtual music ringtones for the mobile phone. The website team needs to make an adjustment to appear the style information, with the mobile application team working to permit customers to search, sneak peek, as well as acquire the ringtones. Both modifications require to be made to the magazine service, but regrettably fifty percent the group is out with the influenza, and the various other fifty percent is stuck identifying a manufacturing failure.

We have a number of choices that don't entail common solutions to prevent this scenario. The Is to simply wait. The website and mobile application teams proceed to something else. Relying on just how vital the function is, or exactly how long the hold-up is most likely to be, this may be fine or it might be a major problem.

You can instead add individuals to the directory team to help them move with their work much faster. The more standard the technology pile as well as configuring idioms in use across your system, the less complicated it is for various other individuals to make modifications in your solutions. The flipside, obviously, as we discussed earlier, is that standardization has a tendency to lower a team's capability to take on the ideal solution for the job, as well as can lead to different kind of ineffectiveness. If the group gets on the various other side of the world, this may be impossible, nevertheless.

One more option could be to divide the directory into a separate basic music catalog and also a ringtone catalog. And the if the adjustment being made to sustain ringtones is rather little. possibility of this being an area in which we will certainly establish heavily in the future is additionally fairly reduced, this may well be early. On the various other hand, if there are 10 weeks of ringtonerelated features stacked up, splitting out the solution can make feeling, with the mobile team taking possession. There is another design that can work well for us, though.

Inner Open Source.

So suppose we've tried our hardest, but we just can not find a way past having a few shared services? At this moment, appropriately welcoming the internal open resource design can make a lot of feeling with regular open resource, a little group of individuals are thought about core committers. They are the custodians of the code. If you desire a modification to an open resource task, you either ask one of the committers to make the adjustment for you, or else you make the change on your own as well as send them a pull demand. The core committers are still in cost of the codebase; they are the owners. Inside the company, this pattern can function well too. Probably individuals that serviced the solution originally are no more on a group with each other; probably they are currently spread throughout the organization. Well, if they still have commit civil liberties, you can discover them and also ask for their assistance, perhaps coupling up with them, or if you have the appropriate tooling you can send them a pull demand.

Role of the Custodians.

We still desire our solutions to be sensible. We desire the code to be of good top quality, and the solution itself to display some sort of uniformity in just how it is created. We additionally desire to make sure that adjustments being made now do not make future scheduled changes a lot harder than they require to be. This means that we require to take on the very same patterns utilized in regular open source internally too, which implies dividing out a team of relied on committers (the core group), and also untrusted committers (people from outside the group sending modifications).

The core group requires to have some method of vetting and approving the adjustments. It requires to make certain the changes are idiomatically consistent-- that is, that they follow the general coding standards of the remainder of the codebase. The individuals doing the vetting are going to have to spend time working with the submitters to ensure the modification is of adequate high quality.

Good gatekeepers placed a great deal of job into this, connecting clearly with the submitters and also encouraging excellent actions. Poor gatekeepers can utilize this as a reason to exert power over others or have spiritual wars concerning arbitrary technical choices. Having seen both collections of behavior, I can inform you one thing is clear: in either case it takes some time. When thinking about permitting untrusted committers to submit adjustments to your codebase, you have to determine if the overhead of being a gatekeeper deserves the trouble: can the core group be doing far better things with the moment it spends vetting spots?


Maturation.


The much less steady or develop a solution is, the more difficult it will certainly be to allow people outside the core team to submit patches. Before the vital back of a solution remains in area, the group might not know what good resemble, and also therefore might battle to know what a great entry resemble. Throughout this phase, the service itself is going through a high degree of modification.

Most open resource tasks often tend to not take entries from a wider team of untrusted committers up until the core of the first variation is done. Adhering to a similar version for your own companies makes good sense. And also is seldom changed-- for if a service is rather mature example, our cart solution-- after that perhaps that is the time to open it up for other contributions.

Tooling.

To ideal sustain an internal open resource model, you'll require some tooling in location. The use of a distributed variation control device with the capability for people to send draw demands (or something similar) is essential. Depending on the size of the organization, you might require tooling to enable a conversation and also the evolution of patch demands; this may or might not mean a full-blown code review system, yet the capability to comment inline on spots is precious. Lastly, you'll need to make it really simple for a committer to develop as well as deploy your software program, as well as make it available for others. Usually this involves having actually well-defined develop and deployment pipes and also centralized artifact repositories.

# CONCLUSION

Microservices are not brand-new. They have marked their existence previously in the form of service-oriented architectures, web services, etc. Clustered together as small independent services, which together formed an application, Microservices originated to conquer monolithic challenges. A structure-based technique and the ideal choice of tools will streamline the building of a microservice application.

With the intervention of several device support, increasing user base, Internet of Things, and interaction with different innovation models, software development has actually ended up being a complicated procedure. Further, it is highly complex when it comes to upgrades. Microservices come as a perfect service to application developers who are forward thinkers.

Microservices is a journey that will impact your organization culturally, technically and operationally. It is the way forward in the advancement of enterprise applications, providing your organization the freedom to adjust quickly according to the future!